THE NOVELS OF ARUN JOSHI

A CRITICAL EVALUATION

BIRENDRA PANDEY

ATLANTIC PUBLISHERS AND DISTRIBUTORS

Published by
ATLANTIC PUBLISHERS AND DISTRIBUTORS
B-2, Vishal Enclave, Opp. Rajouri Garden, New Delhi-27
Phones : 5413460, 5429987

Sales Office
4215/1, Ansari Road, Darya Ganj, New Delhi-02
Phones : 3273880, 3285873, 3280451
Fax : 91-11-3285873
e-mail : info@atlanticbooks.com
web : www.atlanticbooks.com

ISBN 81-7156-935-8

Typeset at
APD Computer Graphics, Delhi

Printed in India at
Nice Printing Press, Delhi

FOREWORD

It is generally an admitted fact that the genesis of the creative process is inseparable from an artist's initial perception but he has to restrict himself to the experience of his own imagination and does not leave the actuality of his shared experience. Truly speaking every novelist must begin by creating for himself a world great or small in which he can honestly believe. It also resembles something already familiar to the experience, thinking and perception of his readers. Thus, it must be a reality which he could imagine, capture and create by giving a consistent form to the shapeless facts of actual human experience. Arun Joshi conforms to this conception of the writer's approach. He feels a need to shape and reshape it. He tries to discover and rediscover the reality which lies hidden in his own life. He reveals a world where man is confronted by the self and the question of his identity. His this effort makes him a great artist of human psychology.

The author, Dr. Birendra Pandey, has attempted an exhaustive study of Arun Joshi's four novels with an insight on his presentation of cultural clashes, rootlessness and meaninglessness of his major characters. The book adds a new dimension to the in-depth study of each novel of Arun Joshi. It is his laudable contribution to Indian Fiction in English.

R.A. SINGH
PROFESSOR
DEPARTMENT OF ENGLISH
VEER KUNWAR SINGH UNIVERSITY
ARA (BIHAR)

ACKNOWLEDGEMENT

I am thankful to a number of literary critics from whom I have received invaluable help in preparing this book on Arun Joshi's Novels. I express my gratitude to Dr. R.A. Singh, Professor and Head, Department of English at S.P. Jain College, Sasaram (Veer Kunwar Singh University, Ara, Bihar) who guided my first steps in research.

I thankfully acknowledge for the burden shared by my wife Shanti and children Pratiksha, Sambhawana, Ankesh and Divya who kept me free from family worries during the writing of this book. I am also obliged to Dr. K.R. Gupta, Managing Director of M/s Atlantic Publishers and Distributors, New Delhi without whom the publication of this book would have been an impossible venture.

BIRENDRA PANDEY

CONTENTS

1

Introduction

English has been the medium of instruction in India for a long time but the Indians have been using English language also for a creative purposes with a serious and systematic attempt in proper historical and cultural context. This has been used to evaluate it as literature. There are critics and commentators in England and America who appreciate Indian Writing in English. Indian English Fiction occupies its proper place in the field of literature. Indian fiction in English in India can't be denied its existence and it has a marked difference. There can be no double standard of criticism for the novels of Indian writers or the English writers. The general problem of Indian Writing in English has received more attention than individual books or authors. It is not irrelevant here to level it original creative writing in English by Indian writers. The wide circulation, the popularity and the mass acceptance of Indian fiction in English has made it acceptable both in India and abroad.

The historical and the political consciousness as well as circumstances combined its forces to give a certain proficiency in the use of English language in India. Right from the 19th Century till now it is an accidental but exceptional in its maturity and richness. The representative writers of Bengal like Toru Dutta, Ramesh Chandra Dutt and Man Mohan Ghosh contributed a lot, but they could not constitute a specific trend. R.N. Tagore and Bankim Chandra Chatterjee helped to survive it. The novelist's main concern is the man in society and his subject matter is the texture of manners and conventions by which social man defines his own identity. The novelists demand direct involvement in values and experiences. The creative activity in his own language enables him for constructive work in other areas of social reformation and political upheaval. It is very interesting to note that the novel emerged at different times in different regions in India with different shape and size specially in Bengali, Hindi, Marathi, Kanada and Malayalam. But it could not catch with the momentum, it needed. Therefore, it is very difficult to evaluate its output till today. The rise of novel is associated with the growth of middle class in the west or in India. A new class of intellectuals appeared to share and communicated this awareness of time and place through the medium of writing fiction in English but it took time to be purposive and pointed. This attempt of the writers was done in phases. Primarily historical romances were written to expose the contemporary evils but later on, the writers voiced their views and concerns openly. They included their still attitude towards the British Government, in justice, cruelty and exploitation of the Indian masses. It was mixed with Gandhism, Marxism, Patriotism and few progressive attitudes to social equality. But with the publication of Mulk Raj Anand's novels *Untouchable* (1935) and *The Coolie* (1936), society changed into action. It was a social protest and regeneration of faith in human dignity. Naturally, the next generation of novelists came to be self-conscious, inward looking and with an analytical approach up to this the second phase of the growth of Indian-English fiction was completed. The journey of Indian English fiction now came to social realism. Though the social outlook changed, the traditional village continued to present a dismal look. But the writings of Mulk Raj Anand, Raja Rao and R.K. Narayan paved the way to make it a definite move in the right direction. Bhawani Bhatacharya and Kamla Markandaya tried to present Indian's mind.

The clash of cultures, Eastern and Western, had been quite a pronounced theme even in the novels of the thirties and the forties. But the writers attitude was then mostly based against the British people. It was in the fifties that the problem of co-existence of different cultures took a huge dimension. It was Mulk Raj Anand, *Two Leaves and a Bud,* who first caricatured English men. But from the novels of the fifties this bitterness disappeared. The American replaced the English presenting the writers with the problem of a new cultural clash. Santha Rama Rao's novel, *Remember the House* (1956) is the first to depict an American pair with sympathy, the possibility of an Indian girl's marriage with an American. Amrita in *Esmond in India* (1958) presents Americans interest in Indian Philosophy and R.P. Jhabvala underlines American's love for the cultural part of India in *The House-holder*. Arun Joshi, in his novel *The Foreigner* confines to the clashes on the existential plain but records with alarming seriousness the danger of the sense of taking position of the mind of those people caught up in the inter-cultural flux.

Indian life even today is by and large guided by traditional values of the joint family system where the rights and duties of each members are well defined. Inter-caste and International marriages are viewed with suspicion and on grounds of cultural differences Jhabvalla *Esmond in India* and Raja Rao's *The Serpent and the Rope* display the disparity of the two cultures. In both cases marriages fail for lack of tolerance. The union between the Indian young men trained in America, and the American Korean girl fails in R.K. Narayan's *The Vendor of Sweets*. The cultural conflict has assumed a vital significance for the Indian novelists in English. When we trace back its history, we have Sarat Kumar Ghosh's novel *The Prince of Destiny*, published in 1909, a novel dealing with inter-cultural theme. In this novel, the hero, the prince of a native Indian state has to choose between the love of an English girl and marriage with an Indian princess. J.M. Ganghuli's *When East and West Meet* (1960), shows the East-West encounter at various depths and meaning. In some novels the west appears as a character and in some others as an attitude or a set of values. But a number of novels have appeared describing the conflicts between the two cultures not on social but on the personal level. In all these cases there is an individual search for identity. A few novelists have shown unabeting interest in the interaction of the two sets of values existing side by side.

There may be other reasons for the Indian writers concerned with the East-West themes but it is no more than a manifestation of the writer's constant awareness of a Western audience. The fact that the Indian novelists in English are generally more acquainted with Western culture seems to have valid reasons for their concerns. Those Indians who have learnt English language through books and are not really connected with their daily life, are not seriously affected by the Western values, but for that who have a more extensive exposure and confrontation of these two kinds of values, is their major concern. For those writers this confrontation has not resulted in any tension but they simply sustain their view of life. D.F. Karka, whose novels are set in England, display his intimate knowledge of English life and culture but it makes no contribution either to English or Indian literature. His novel *Just Flesh* (1951) has British characters but no grips or reality. In his last novel *We Never Die* (1943) he handles a theme based on an Indian village.

There is another group of novelists dealing with inter-cultural tension but it does not seriously affect the course of events in their fiction. R.K. Narayan and K. Nagarjun are the two novelists who write about life as it is known to them. Their novels are set in the particular areas of the earth — Malgudi and Kedaram. But they never indulge in generalization about what is Indian and what is Western. Manohar Malgaonkar deals with this conflict with a sense of justice. He describes inefficiency, servility, dishonesty, sense of inferiority and integrity which are typically Indian. In his four novels *Distant Drum* (1960), *Combat of Shadows* (1962), *The Princes* and *A Bend in the Ganges* (1966), Malgaonkar, with the help of Indian characters, makes a difference in race and nationality. There is a contrast between the two cultures — Indian and English.

But apart from these writers the majority of Indian writers in English try to seek a creative challenge in this tension between two civilizations. This duality of culture may be a source of strength to the writers or it may be serious handicap because writing about societies of different values a writer may have a different level of internal change, therefore, it can't be an easy task.

The conflict undoubtedly offers major problems for the study of anthroplogists or the sociologists. European culture has filtered down in Indian and British cultures. But the complexity is never superficial. Like American culture, Indian culture has its own distinctive part. In both cases the attitude towards Europe is diverse and complex. The confrontation with the West for the discovery of Indian self and contemporary motives finds expression in Indian novels of B. Rajan. The protagonists return home after a period spent abroad forms an important incident. Raja Rao's *The Serpent and the Rope* begins with Ramaswami's coming back to India after spending some years in France, and his metaphysical definition of the re-discovered country. Santha Rama Rao's young heroine Baba Goray has just returned from school in England as *Remember the House* opens. In most of these cases here is an autobiographical element of the persons who have returned but generally autobiography does not interfere with the internal design of the art. In each case the protagonists awareness of two civilization intensifies his concern with his own identity. They are all in search of their true image and in each case the novels ends with the resolution of their dilemma through a definite action.

In this distinction between Eastern and Western values, it is very difficult to demarcate the tensions between the two traditions available in India as they oversimplify action and conflict — but we try to make a tentative definition of the two values. The central conflict between two ideas of life in B. Ranjan's *The Dark Dancer* the West appears in person and the narrator's American friend who makes happiness her goal in life represents one side of the conflict. The other side does not have a similar concrete personification. The heroine's mother is an embodiment of two Indian values. The narrator Baba Goray who is infatuated with the American way of life finds the ideal of enjoyment, success and happiness all desirable. The difference between the two modes of life is within their frame-work of happiness. In Attia Hussain's *Sun Light on a Broken Column*, the conflict does not resolve neatly along East-West lines, though, the heroine's quest for her personal destiny itself is a result of the impact of the West on her. Laila's journey disintegrates from the acceptance of traditional family values to questioning and rebellion. She takes the decision of marrying Ammer against the will or her family. Unlike the heroine of Santha Rama Rao, Laila chooses to defy traditions and in the conflict between the society and individual, her individuality, wins. Attia Hussains's heroine also follows the same pattern. In Kamala Markanadaya's *Some Inner Fury,* Meera recalls the happiness, Gulmohar's and peace of her father's home. The conflict, between the two cultures are spelled out in Nayantara Sehgal's first novel *'A Time to be Happy'*. The protagonist Sanad Shivapal is the sterco-type of a particular social class. His self pity, essence of alienations and rootlessness is very common in Indian novels in English. His wife Kusum conforms to the type of idealized Indian womanhood and is equal to premela of *Some Inner Fury* and Kamala of *The Dark Dancer.*

With Nayantara Sehgal, Anita Desai and Arun Joshi Indian English novel makes a distinct departure. The novelists have no shift from the outer world to the inner recesses of mind and heart. They are passionately concerned with the dilemma of human loneliness. The characters of Nayantara Sehgal are no more sex creatures rather they are solitary individuals trying to combat loneliness. In Anita Desai they are completely strangers and unable to communicate. In these fictions the crisis is born out of matrimonial discord, the lack of understanding between man and woman.

Arun Joshi presents different facets of crisis in modern man's life. The image in all his novels is an image of foreigner. His characters are not only in the dilemma of dual cultures but lively pictures of alienations. His Sindi is a foreigner wherever he goes. His Billy retreats to find life essence in Bilasia. His Ratan Rathore is torn between guilt and confession. His Som Bhashkar is lost in the Labyrinth of death and life, existence and reality, doubt and faith.

All the four novels of Arun Joshi are set in search of reality. Joshi has not only attracted a large number of readers, writers and reviewers but he has also received appreciation from Indian and foreign critics.

The Present study of Arun Joshi's novels is a humble attempt to assign the novelist his due place among the Indian writers in English. For this a revaluation of his novels is necessary and efforts have been made to deal with all the major aspects of the novelists achievements but the focus is centered on his interpretation of the clash of cultures, that is the spontaneous overflow of Joshi's psyche. Joshi has evolved a style and thematic approach with an understanding for the young people. On the whole the emphasis is on the clashes of cultures and the novelistic technique developed by him. Since no work has till this day been done on this aspect of Joshi's art, the present contribution, though a humble one, is original in nature.

2

Warring Cultures of East and West

Arun Joshi is such an artist who takes us to the surface of the East and the West. In all his four novels we have descriptions of warring cultures of East and West. *The Foreigner* by Joshi presents the two cultures side by side. In The *Foreigner Sindi* Oberoi, the protagonist is a product of cross roads of the West and the East. His dilemma is socio-psychological. Oberoi is born of an English mother and an Indian father. He is brought up by his uncle in Kenya. He is educated in East Africa, London and America. He is deprived of parental love and has indifference towards them. In an indifferent tone he tells Mr. Khemba about them :

> For the hundredth time I related the story of
> those strangers whose only reality was a couple
> of wrinkled and cracked photographs.[1]

He remembers those days when they were killed in an aircrash and he needed them most for the growth of his personality. He does not believe the tragedy :

> I said they had been killed in an air crash
> near cairo and that I had been brought up
> by an uncle in Kenya I wanted to add that
> I did not particularly miss them, that it was
> too long ago for me to remember but I
> thought that might be misconstrued (p. 11).

Sindi feels some kind of security with his uncle but death of his uncle makes him miserable and forces him to lead life of a foreigner. He thinks himself insecure and without an anchor :

---

1. Arun Joshi, *The Foreigner,* Hind Pocket Books, New Delhi.

> I had not felt like that when my uncle was living. It was not that I loved him very much or anything — as a matter of fact we rarely exchanged letters — but the thought that he moved about in that small house on the outskirts of Nairobi gave me a feeling of having an anchor. After his death the security was destroyed (pp. 61-62).

Sindi Oberoi is denied parental love, family affection and cultural roots. He grows into a wayward man and finally becomes a wanderer alien to his own culture. He has no longer any sense of security because of his isolation from his own family and the society. His cut out relation and his sense of being an outsider remains to be static. His mental agonies and predicament can be seen in the following lines :

> But you at least knew what made an ass of a man; we do not even know that you had a clear cut system of morality, a caste system that laid down all you had to do. You had a God you had roots in the soil you lived upon, look at me. I have no roots. I have no system of morality. What does it mean to me if you call me an immoral man. I have no reason to be one thing rather than another. You ask me why I am not ambitious; well, I have no reason to think of it I don't even have a reason to live (pp. 135-136).

Though he has some mission, some purpose, some desire in life but he has withdrawn himself from action. He desires to be a saint, he wants to escape pain, he tries in many ways but all fails. He wants to do something to get out of attachment but finding no answers to these strange questions, he is internally hurt. He records the pain of these internal wounds. This state of self-pity is obvious in the following lines :

> There were things, I wanted, only I didn't know how to get them. I wanted the courage to live as I wanted; the courage to live without desire and attachment, I wanted peace and perhaps capacity

> to love. I wanted all these. But above all, I wanted to conquer pain. What could I have done with the directorship of a Company if the ball of pain still hung around my neck like a dead albatross I wanted an answer to the questions that my suffering had left with me like swollen carcasses strewn on river banks after a flood. Only after I knew what my purpose was, could I begin to fulfil it (pp. 138).

Sindi Oberoi has been an alien throughout his life right from his life in Kenya, London and Boston he undergoes various changes and varied experiences. While in Kenya once he thinks for suicide and when he comes to London his dull roots stir to a little life in his relationship with Anna and Kathy. A girl like Anna seeks to find out her lost youth and live for Oberoi but in response he gives her a sense of illusion and shows his liking for Kathy. These experiences and the burden of broken relationship disturb him intensely. Up till now his detachment creates an illusion in his life. He knows intimately the relationship with June and Babu in Boston. He takes a new lease of life when he opts for June, an American girl. His relationship goes deeper but his defences of detachment crumble down when he learns that she wants to love, marry and create a home for her. We have her sense of sacrifice and love for the mystical in her desire revealed hereunder :

> I like meeting people from different countries, especially people from Asia. They are so much gentler and deeper than others, don't you think? (p. 32).

In the split personality of Sindi Oberoi, Arun Joshi surveys the prejudices and illusions of the East and the West. He investigates this point also through an American girl June and Indian boy Babu. June likes to meet with foreign students and the parties orgnaised by the foreign student office and International Students Association also helps her to know others culture. In one of such meetings she meets Sindi Oberoi and comes very close to him. But on his part Sindi maintains a kind of detachment towards her. At this stage Babu enters the scene fascinated by the fantasies and illusions of much publicised glamorous dreamland of America. He finds America a paradise for those seeking free sex. Babu is an Indian boy who does not know the intensity of attachment outside the country with foreign cultures quite unknown to him. June knows that she is in love with Sindi but cannot refuse to oblige Babu. She even does not want to make it known to Babu and in this way her dilemma intensifies and her sense of sexual gratification tears her personality from within. Finally, she comes to compromise with her tension and Sindi gives an account of her love with him :

> We made love with a strange fierceness that was as excruciating in its pleasure as it was painful. And then just after the final moment her body was thrown into a paroxysm of spasms. She shuddered under me in a thousand convulsions gasping for breath. She bit into my shoulder until blood came out and then suddenly I discovered that she was crying. I put my arms around her and tried to calm her down. She bit her lip and tried to hide her face in the pillow. Then something seemed to break within her and she burst into uncontrollable sobs (p. 125).

Against this cultural background Sindi Oberai has also his dilemmas. He cultivates a sense of detachment to overcome his painful memories of the past. He wants to avert the tragedy of June and Babu when he feels his responsibilities and involvement in it. He soon realizes his sense of detachment and objectivity when he finds values in life :

> to speculate about these things objectively not realising that objectivity was just another form of vanity.
>
> begun to see the fallacy in it. Detachment consisted of right action and not escape from it (p. 119).

When this crisis he overcomes and finishes his studies, Sindi Oberoi decides to come over to India. In India he has also a kind of affection about life, vanities and morality. He sees Mr. Khemka's industrial estate based on manupulations.

This thinking of Sindi Oberoi reaches the depths of human problems of socio-cultural existence. The word foreigner finds a symbolical value in the larger context of human existence. It provides ample opportunity for the study of cross cultures. We also come to know individual and human problems against the background of different cultures. It is not simply the question of cultures but Sindi's twice removal from his country of birth, therefore, he is alien everywhere. He wishes to achieve equipose through non-attachment in vain. It is his delusion that he can live uninvolved and unaffected. His advice to June breaks his emotional tie and proves to be a self-delusion when he says :

> Marriage would not help, June. We are alone, both you and I that is the problem. And our aloneness must be resolved from within. You can't send two persons through a ceremony and expect that their aloneness will disappear (p. 126).

Sindi's feeling of insecurity, and meaninglessness of life compels him to defend the delusion, he is passing through a crisis as he has a different view. He says it inevitable, sad and painful and also a deliberate act of madness :

> It is different with me. I have no delusions to bank upon. I can't marry you because I am incapable of doing so. It would be like going deliberaltely mad. It is inevitable that our delusions will break us up sooner or later (p. 120).

Here Sindi gives a false image and seems to be a self-deciever with the ideas that he has developed about detachement and delusion. His ideas of marriage is only once in a life time. He advises Babu when Babu is in a delicate position :

> Woman are desirable creatures but they can also hurt you. We all make use of each other even

> though we do not want to. In your part of the world you marry only once in a lifetime. It is quite a serious matter. Don't just rush into a wrong thing for a temporary need (p. 117).

When Oberoi comes to India just to inform the sad death of Babu, he finds himself an alien sitting in Khemka's palacial house. At this meeting with Khemka's family and specially with his daughter Sheila. He is unable to control the passions within him. He does not forget the foreign background during the conversation he narrates his feeling outside the world :

> I was considered quite a misfit. My foreign background stood against me. Nobody hated me. I was too insignificant for that sort of thing. But I suspect they considered me a little too causal even though some of them envied me a bit for my lightheartedness (p. 15).

Money ruins life but without money a man cannot have a station in life. Oberoi has also observed these facts of life. It is human's weakness to have greed for money irrespective of cultures while he examines two facts of life — poverty and riches, — he easily differentiates between the two. His long travel from one country to another and his wide experiences with the cultures of different countries has given him internal satisfaction to think about the life of the poor and the rich alike while he says :

> I had read much of inequality in India; now I could see it masquerade as company law and the amendements of paraliment. I had no morals to apply one way or the other, but that fat man left me with a distinct feeling of being out of place. We were looking for two different worlds (p. 16).

To Sindi Oberoi, there are cultural differences everywhere. In America everyone is busy every time. No one is free to entertain any one but in Delhi there are people they can entertain foreigners. The Indian culture to him is a different culture. This can be clearly seen in the conversation between Oberoi and Babu :

> Well, just because they are foreigners. If we meet any Americans in Delhi we take great interest in them, don't we (p. 20).

There are also differences of cultures in respect of marriages. In India marriage is an institution. Majority of people like traditional marriage than the marriages based on advertisement. But in American culture marriage is a sort of temporary association for sexual gratification. It is not binding on the partners for life long. It may break on the discretion of either of two. Those who visit America and accept American culture does not care for the sanctity of marriage. Babu has also the same experience when he says :

> What is the good of coming to America if one is not to play around with girls? (p. 22).

In America, Sindi does not mix with the culture of the people there. When he has an opportunity to attend a party or to go to public path, or to buy a ticket, he remains himself as an *ex-officio* host or an alien. He has the only feeling of alienation, loneliness and insecurity :

> Except for the bartender and me there was not a soul in the room who was not dancing or talking or beating his feet to the music. It is remarkable how you can be in a crowded room like that and still feel lonely, like you were sitting in your own tomb (p. 23).

At times he passes through psycho-analysis. He blames American cultures for disturbances in his life, the disorder he undergoes the obsession he faces. His faith in God dispells the mysticism which the American culture has given him to learn. He realises his position as an outsider in America. In a disgusted tone he minimises the burden of culture in the following lines :

> I was full of love and sadness at the same time. Even if I loved her and she loved me it would mean nothing, nothing that one could depend upon. I was not the kind of man one could love; I had learnt that long ago (p. 38).

Oberoi is a foreigner but he knows the reality of life in America. The superficiality, the meaninglessness and his emotional breath throughout combines experience of his journey from one country to another. He suffers a lot but he never takes it otherwise. He maintains :

> There is no end to suffering, no end
> to the struggle between good and evil (p. 41).

Sindi, June and Babu have different roots and all of them are trying for existence in other's culture. Babu is quite a different sort of boy. He has his roots in Indian soil, but wings in America. He loves June, decides to marry her but his conventional morality comes in the way when he discovers that she in in love with others also. He is haunted by jealousy and suspicion but he can't resist his temptation for June. He tries to forget his roots and wants to destroy the process of changes that may occur here. He gives June all she needs but she is also in a reckless condition. She dangles between Babu and Oberoi. The philosophy of detachment and temporiness of love does not suit her. She pleads her case with Sindi :

> I had wanted to belong to you, but you did not want it. You are so self-sufficient there is hardly any place for me in your life — except perhaps as a mistress. Babu, on the other hand, was on the edge of a breakdown — all still is for that matter. He loves me more than he loves himself — that's more than what can be said for you. In return I am prepared to give him all that I have (p. 158).

When Babu comes to know that Sindi is in love with her without lust or passion but simply to help her find herself, he decides to kill himself. This false detachment of Sindi drives him to death. In his death oriental innocence he is destroyed in the strange ways of the Western culture. After his death June also dies. Her death symbolises cultural lag. The two cultures of East and West hardly meet. In comparison of June, Babu is a simple character having Indian roots and middle class values, while June is a complex character. Sindi Oberoi is responsible for the death of both, though he feels a sense of guilt and self-contradiction, he is once again before the readers naked in the hands of existence. He feels like an insecure man and harbours a deep rooted feeling of unreality. He wants to justify his identity through his contacts with others and loses both individuality and identity. He suffers the psychosis of engulfment. His relationship with Anna, Kathy and June fails as he cannot make out a complete union in any case. His dialogue with June gives an account of his fear psychosis which he tries to hide :

> I said I didn't quite know except that whatever I had seen so far in life seemed to indicate that marriage was more often a lust for possession than anything else. People got married just as they bought new cars. And then they gobbied each other up. But marriage is also love, is not it, June said. I said I imagined it was since everybody said so, but as far as I was concerned, love that wanted to possess was more painful than no love at all. One should be able to love without wanting a lot more harm than good. One should be able to detach oneself from the object of one's lone (p. 67).

Sindi is pre-occupied with the sense of possession of a girl like June. While he tries to preserve his identity he is terrified with the fear of being possessed. He fears to be united in marriage because he sees his existence doomed. He works on the theory that "one should be able to love without wanting to possess." He has not courage to make a meaningful lesson :

> All love — whether of things, or persons, or one self — was illusion and all pain sprang from this illusion. Love begot greed and attachment, and it led to possession. Absence of love does not mean hatred. Hatred is just another form of love. There is another way of loving. You can love without attachment, without desire. You can love

> without attachment to the objects of your love. You can love without fooling yourself that the things you love are indispensable either to you or to the world. Love is real only when you know that what you love must one day die (p. 170).

In between attachment and detachment he finally understands that deachment does not mean an escape or an alientation, it means involvement, devotion and sacrifice. He surrenders to himself as an existential hero and settles with the business, with Sheila and with herself, Dr. Hari Mohan Prasad rightly remarks :

> From Boston to Delhi has been a journey from alientation to arrival, from selfishness to sacrifice, from an anomic responsible to himself to a member of mankind, from being to becoming (p. 43).

The clash of culture in *The Strange Case of Billy Biswas* is something different than that of *The Foreigner*. Sindi of *The Foreigner* and the Billy of *The Strange Case of Billy Biswas* are two different poles. Billy's quest is deeper than the quest Sindi Oberoi has undertaken. Billy's concern is not intellectual like that of Sindi. It is because of his deep roots in family, traditions and a fixed set of values. He has a standing and that is the position of an Indian saint who is less concerned with external world than the internal with self realization in life. Billy's case is very much like the case of these Indian saints in the final resolution of life. The novelist paints Billy vividly in the following lines :

> If life's meaning lies not in the glossy surfaces of our pretensions but in those dark mossy labyrinths of the soul that languish forever, hidden from the dazzling light of the sun, then I do not know of any man who sought it more doggedly and, having received a signal, abandoned himself so recklessly to its call. In brief, I know of no other man who so desperately pursued the tenuous thread of existence to its bitter end, no matter what trails of glory or shattered hearts he left behind in his turbulent wake (p. 8).

Billy is seen first in New York attending a mid-western university for a summer course at Columbia. He is introduced to the friends by an Engineer, Anthropologist. Billy is crazy and he responded by Indian standards but he comes from the upper class Indian society. In America he lives with Indians and negroes. One can find British accent in his speech because of his school-education in England. He is the son of ex-Indian Ambassador to the European countries but his deep roots in the wild culture and his association with the negroes in America tells us the other side of his life.

Billy has a very good ancestral background. His family had originally come from Bengal. His grandfather had been the Prime Minister in Orissa and his father practised law at Allahabad and Delhi. While Billy was in America his father was a Judge of Supreme Court in India. Billy has sound knowledge of both Indian society and culture. The primitive man interested him very much. He also wanted to organise his entire life on that pattern. He has a peculiar liking for things :

> His output consisted of a most incongruent mixture of book reviews, poems, fanatstic short stories and some very crudite essays on the science of anthropology (p. 14).

The conversation between two sophisitcated and cultured minds Billy Biswas and Tuula Lindgren is significant. Tuula who had come to America for advance training in Psychiatric social work. Tuula is going to work in a mental hospital in Topeka and Billy wants her close contact as a tutor in Anthropology. Tuula asks his choice for a job. He puts it as follows :

> The otherside. You know what I mean, don't you? Must of us are aware only of the side — on which we are born, but there is always the othersides the valley beyond the hills; the hills beyond the valley (pp. 18-19).

Billy belongs to a well-to-do family and that is why he has to face much difficulties. He is unable to fulfil his wishes because he does not want to tie up the secret of his wish fulfilment. He feels something within and he has not courage to divulge it. He is afraid of it. Tuula Lindgren's remark is apt here :

> Billy feels something inside him, but he is not yet sure. A great force, unkraft, a..... a primitive force. He is afriad of it and tries to suppress it. But it is very strong in him, much stronger than you or me. It can explode any time (p. 23).

Meena Chatterjee who belongs to a Bengali family comes in contact with Billy and she gives her identification entirely in English accent. She is very talkative. She gives a lengthy philosophy of horse riding and later on she goes on the talk of horsemen and sportsmen. At first sight and in first meeting Billy discloses :

> Things might have been different, Romi, if that wretched storm had not come up when it did. You see what I mean, don't you? I did not and I told him so; but then there were many things that I did not see which Billy saw and which, step by step, led him to the only end that awaits those who see too much (pp. 39-40).

On marraige proposal with Meena, Billy has not his self-confidence. He does not know about Indian social life. He wants to take advice of his friend, old chap, who is now an I.A.S. Officer and geeting training at Simla. His friend knows enough of the world and he is aware of the men who wants to impart confidence but for Billy his general ideas are outweighed. As a matter of fact there is a great change in the atmosphere. Old chap discourses to Billy about the importance of a wife necessary socially, sexually and for a future life. According to Hindu Mythology a man's duty is to marry and reproduce. He analyses the needs for marriage in this way :

> I offered him the usual amalgum of Western pragmatism (a wife is so necessary socially, sexually, for a fuller life and Hindu dharma. Man's duty to marry and reproduce; there is a time for everything) that is the conventional wisdom of the Indian middle class (p. 42).

Billy has sharp inhumanly eyes. Once with his friend Mr. Old Chap, he is crossing by a cottage at right. A girl's voice going over the notes of the Sargam attracts him. It affects his emotions, the emotions that one tends to associate with a great predicament, looking up at the window Billy is delight to have a very nice voice mixed up with Pancham tuning fork; while Mr. Old Chap asks about his interst in music, he replies :

> Every Bengali child is expected to go through his cultural catechism although I must admit at one stage I was rather fond of it (p. 44).

On the cutural lag Billy's views are totally different to his parents. For his mother, recommendations for an anthroplogist to be a millionaire is simply by acting as middle man between tribes and numerous gods. This fastidious idea pinches Billy. By chance the murder case of Krishna is to be judged by his father. A case of human sacrifice takes place in the heart of Delhi. A middle aged government clerk and his wife commits murder of a twelve year old boy to propitiate the goddess Kali for their son. At this time for their defence premeditation has been introduced but the concept of temporary insanity or delusion had been introduced by Billy's father. Both differ in their approach to the cultures leading to the sacrifice of the boy to please goddess Kali. When Billy's father denies the plea of temporary insanity made in this case, Billy defines the term 'premeditation' used by his father earlier and his arguments in defence breaks his father's dilemmas :

> For one whole week the man plans and premeditates, arranges for the butcher's knives, silver chalices, sandal wood, ghee, etc. persuades the wretched vagrant to spend the night at his home. How could it be temporary insanity? (p. 53).
>
> *　　*　　*　　*
>
> Pre-meditation, as you use the term, is the concept of this world, the every day world of government offices, power breakdowns, stock exchanges, etc., you do agreement with me that this is the only world for which your laws are made, do not you? (pp. 53-54).

He cites other examples in his favour, which also happens in the world. It is of global phenomenon and it is also a·part of world culture :

> Similar cases have been reported from Africa, Indonesia, Japan, from even a country like Sweden. As far as India is concerned, there are enough such cases to fill a thousand-page volume. Look up the court records of any of tribal agencies, and you will know what I mean (p. 54).

Billy is not satisfied with Meena because he is in great spirits. He dislikes the commerical people like his parents and wife Meena. He wants permanent peace but he is unable to find it in the surroundings in which he lives. He shows annoyance although she is his wife, he wants to be in a company far from these people with whom he has nothing to adjust. He shows his ever inclination to Meena. Meena shows her emotions fluttering like a crushed butterfly :

> If I even open my mouth I bore you. If I speak what is in my mind, I am being silly. Why did you have marry such a boring silly girl. Oh, God! I wish I were dead (pp. 80-81).

A large envelope is handed over to Mr. Old Chap from Tuula Lindgren by Dr. Kundt of a Swedish Embassy in Delhi which is full of letters by Billy to Tuula that were written about a year after his return to India and the last nearly six months before his disappearance. These letters make an investigative approach and also shows the mental abnormality of Mr. Billy Biswas arising out of cultural clashes in his mind. He is struggling with himself and wants to go to a peaceful world of imagination where he could be capable of realising the real meaning of life. He hates those cultured men who like busy earning and spending of money. Some remarkable extracts of his letters are sure to throw light on his views about the people :

> I see a roomful of finely dressed men and women seated on downy sofas and while I am looking at them under my very nose, they turn into kennel

> of dogs yawning (their larger teeth showing) or snuggling against each other or holding whisky glasses in their furred paws... I sometimes wonder whether civilization is anything more making and spending of money. What else the civilized men do? What need would there be of psychiatrists research foundations, learned societies, great scholars, scientists, ministerial adviser, Ambassadors, generals, had the world not initially been hung on this peg of money (pp. 96-97).

Billy finds peace and happiness in the woods and with the tribals. The sounds and smells of a lonely forest life echo in his ears even if he comes back to a city life :

> When I returned from an expedition, it is days before I can shake off their sounds and smells of the forest. The curious feeling trails me everywhere that I am a visitor from the wilderness to the marts of the big city and not the other way round (pp. 96-97).

He likes to live with the tribals on Maikala Hills. He wants to be primitive pilgrim, a wanderer in the woods, a self seeker with the tribal folk. He describes his strange journey. He expresses his thoughts towards tribals, their appearance, their living and their management also. Here a helpless tribal finds a beautiful pen picture :

> On one of my visits I saw in a village a dog and an old man, two skeletons that managed barely to crawl, licking at the water trickling from the spout of an empty tanker. The old man, his eyes closed with exhaustion, was obviously too weak to push the dog away. I hoped never again to have to witness a sight such as that (p. 100).

The conflict of cultures arises in his mind. He leads a life of feuherer. The complexity of his thoughts compels him to think a lot for his being in that very society where he is disappointed to reach his goal. He looks like a stranger. He writes to Tuula :

> It seems, my dear Tuula, that we are swiftly losing what is known as one's grip on life. Why else this constant blurring of reality? Who am I? Who are my parents? My wife? At times I took at them, sitting at the dinner table, and for a passing moment I can not decide who they are or what accident of creation has brought us together (p. 97).

Billy is satisfied with the tribal's culture. He is happy because he is far from the world that hangs on the peg of money. Here he is found talking about the supernatural, violent death, trees, earth, ruin, dust storms, rivers, mods of the forest, animals, dance, singing and a lot about women and sex. Bilasia consoles his despair and makes his life happy.

> I told my Sajan : sing to me all night. Life was meant to be sung and we were meant to be singers. But my Sajan went away. O, my Sajan went away (p. 117).

Billy, now, is going to be attached with the hills, forests, tribal people and each and every objects of the Nature. He has a quest for self-realisation with the missing part of his soul. His sense of corruption hunts him. He, sitting outside his tent in the forest, is attracted at the call of natural objects for the primitive world. His mind moves towards the primitive life :

> They all seemed to be waiting and watching and staring at me. It was as though I was not Bimal Biswas, graduate of Columbia, the only son of a Supreme Court Judge, husband of Meena Biswas, and father of a handsome child...It was as though I were not all this but the first man on earth facing the earth's first night ... come to our primitive world the would sooner or later overcome the works of man. Come we have waited for you...Come, come, come, come. Why do you want to go back? Why do you want to go back? This is all there is on earth. This and the woman waiting for you in the little hut at the

> bottom of a hill. You thought New York was real. You thought New Delhi was your destination. How mistaken you have been! (pp. 120-121).

This interest of Billy in primitivism is not an interest cultivated one but it is inborn, while he is in New York he chooses to live in the places where the negroes live. He has been sent to read Engineering but he chooses Anthropology. It appears from his choice that he has a dislike for an organised life or the life of a cultured man now. His standard of living in Harlem apartment also shows his disliking for an organised life. In any of the indoor games he does not display dexterity when his attention is drawn to this fact. He tried to impress Romi that he is in a trance and getting inspirations vitality from the sources unknown to him. She is very close to Tuula because she has primitive force in her and far from the commerical life of modern civilization. In her company he feels plenty of happiness. He proposes to study the mental working of deranged people because he finds more meaning in their reactions than in those cultured men. Study of Anthropology brings him closer to the life he likes to lead. In the first stage he needed stimulous like alcohal or dance or folk song or drum beating to transport him to the life he dreams of but now he has clear visions without any stimulous. He narrates his vision in the following lines :

> It would be like a great blinding flash during which I would be totally unaware of anything else. And invariably it left me with the old depressing feeling that something has gone wrong with my life. I was not where I belonged (p. 181).

Sometimes Billy complains of hypocricy and dishonesty. In him a sense of feeling gradually developes that he has been turned, dishonest and hypocrite. He is receiving his soul at the cost of material joys and pleasures but in the picnic party he does not tolerate the remarks of his friend that 'the banjaras are thieves and their wives are whores.' That remarks of his friend shakes his faith. He gets ready to marry Meena but she cannot engage his soul altogether to satisfy his inner urge.

Billy is a stranger to the civilized society therefore he has an intense hatred for them. To him this civilization is a monster. It is not the civilization but the degradation of human soul. Simply earning money and spending it is not the civilization. Our thinkers, philosophers and spiritualists can only complicate the culture. His dislike for money is intense. He is attracted to Tuula because she has no hankering after money. This is also the case with Bilasia. It is due to these pulls and pressures that marriage does not unite his body or soul. Meena fails to satisfy his thirst. Romi finds him a changed man. Meena does not see him like the man she had married Romi discovers bitter secret in his transformation :

> It was as though some part of him had gone on strike. All my words simply sank upon his listless mind without so much as causing a ripple. Gone was the staggering intelligence, the spectroscopic interests, the sense of humour. He had either turned banal, something I had seen happen often enough, or, unknown to us, he was turned upon some obscure segment of himself, fretting out a bitter secret, setting an old score (p. 70).

Billy's vision are stronger than the sense of harmony in his surrounding, family life and the life with his wife Meena. He gets introverted, he retires within himself, he opts for the life of a pilgrim. He feels a gap of communication between his wife and himself. Simply sex can't satisfy him to release his tension so he leaves Meena's company for many months — as Meena is a product of modern civilization. Billy needs some one who can share his thought and apply himself to inject a new lease of life to him. He is now attracted to Rima Kaul. She loves him passionately. She is something better than Meena. She shares his feelings :

> Oh, how misunderstood you are, my poor boys, I know how you feel. Those who harass you should be put to death straightway it was this that I was really looking for (p. 18).

He is fed up with the strangers, unresponsive people, statue like Meena and corruption of soul in which Rima Kaul is living. While he gets a glimpse of Bilasia in Dhunia's hut her glimsps gives him a powerful pull. The charm of Bilasia is not sensual but it gives him thrill and also overpowers him. He finds the right woman who can quench his thirst, enlighten his senses and save him from corruption and material civilization. He can now renounce Meena, Rima and the civilized world. This transformation of Billy is not the transformation of sex, or sympathy or sublimation but it is a mixing of self. Bilasia fulfils his choice of life :

> Her enormous eyes, only a little foggier with drink, pourced out a sexuality that was nearly as primeval as the forest that surrounded them (p. 141).

Thus, Billy meets Bilasia and unifies himself with her and culture. He finds his real self with her and gets liberation from his own corrupt culture. He proves himself the saviour God of the Tribals. To this aspect of his changes Dhunia tells Romi :

> He is like rain on parched lands, like balm on a wound. These hills have not seen the like of him since the last of our kings passed away (pp. 159-60).

The characters of Arun Joshi possess double inheritence. His Sindi Oberoi is a product of cultural multiplicity, his Billy carries both legacy of urban aristocracy and tribal primitivism. His Ratan Rathore has divided soul. He finally becomes a careerist. He is tempted by women, drinks and easy life. He comes in contact with Himmat Singh to clear defective war-materials and surrenders to his persuations. Though Ratan Rathore in *The Apprentice*, Arun Joshi conceives the social drama against the background of Gandhian values. Ratan sees no glamor in heroism. He finds changed values, truth, honesty, hard labour and character — all are meaningless to him. His mother also tells him :

> Man without money was a man without worth. Many things were great in life, but the greatest of them all was money (20).

Thus, the parallel cultures of the rich and the poor moves in his mind. He feels that money culture has poisoned the entire society. Money makes friends and it succeeds where all else fails. When the Sheikh tells Ratan about all these, Ratan without any hesitation agrees that corruption has been nationalised in India. He speaks with confidence :

> A bribe could get you a bed in a Hospital, a place to burn you dead. Doctors had a fee to give false certificates. Magistrates for false judgements. For a sum of money politicians changed sides. For a larger sum they declared wars. Bribery was accepted by factory, inspectors, bank agents and college profesors, by nurses, priests and chartered accountants; by all those who acted in the public interest. Men took the bribes to facilitate the seduction of their wives; women for seduction of other woman (p. 142).

The clash of Culture in *The Apprentice* is different from that of *The Strange Case of Billy Biswas.* Billy is not a victim of corrupt society but Ratan Rathor is concerned with corruption. Billy rejects the material civilizations and money-mindedness. Bilasia has nothing to do with money or money culture or materialism but in *The Apprentice* Arun Joshi presents omnipresent corruption in the country. It is the story of the social sickness and sufferings of Ratan Rathor. As a village boy Ratan considers life to be a beautiful sacrifice but the hardships of his life show the sense of insecurity in him. He is nervous for getting a job when he does not find it in the village. He wants to be distinguished from other village boys like the brigadier. He goes to Delhi in search of job, meets all his friends and relatives but finally he suffers privation. He does not want too much but a job to earn his livelihood. He strives hard but he is rejected everywhere. Ratan Rathor, though educated, polished, intelligent and cultured wanders from office to office in search of job. Here his deeply rooted culture of an Indian village boy gets a major change.

He narrates :

> I had become, at the age of twenty-one hypocrite and a lair, in short, a sham.... From morning till night I told more lies than truths. I had become a master faker (p. 128).

He has breakdown of faith and nobility, justice and hard labour. At least a steno friend helps him to get a job as an office assistant, whree he deals with the purchase of war-materials. Here he is ready for departure from his father's ideals. He is no more idealist or heroic about him. Here he longs for a career which his father disliked with all alertness and competence he pleases his Superintendent. Though Ratan Rathor has a long series of compromises in his life but at every compromise his conscience bites him. He is restless, sleepless and unable to ignore the making of his career. He is terrified by the uncertainties of life. Still corruption has not entered into the last layer of his soul, as he has become a thick skinman :

> I am thick-skin now, a thick-skin and a wash out but, believe me, my friend, I too have had thoughts such as these, but what was to be done? One had to live. And, to live, one had to make a living. And, how was a living to be made except through careers (p. 41).

Thus, we find that at every shift in his life Ratan Rathor has a deviating tendency but this deviation from the ideals torments him. He has to suppress the voice of his soul. Falsity, hypocricy and corruption are the things which teach him to be a faker. The Western culture teaches him to disbelieve God and God's existence. He suffers within :

> And all these years this terrible loneliness, something that you may not suspect by looking at me, something that none has even suspected. How, all these years, carrying them in secret, like a thief close to my heart, until their blazes have turned upon me and turned me to ashes (pp. 74-75).

In *The Last Labyrinth* two opposite cultures inflict Som Bhaskar. He inherits the afflications of both of them. Born and brought up in India Som Bhaskar has his studies abroad. He has his education at some of the best Universities of the world and has also spent many years outside India. Therefore, it is natural to him to imbibe something of Western outlook. He has come to rely on reason, scientific temper, materialistic outlook, intellectual appetite and other gifts of the west. In fact inflictions of contradictions are in his blood. The hierarchy of his family tradition is that his grand-father is a happy carefree man, on the other hand his father is a scientist and desirous to know the mystry of the universe. He wants to know the relationships between cause and effect. Som Bhaskar works on this footsteps on his father and forefather but he is also thirsty for knowledge. His mother has unflinching faith in religion as she suffers from Cancer. She has the only faith that Lord Krishna can only cure her. She invites Tuka Ram, the great devotee to Krishna.

A close examination of Bhaskar's personality reveals insecurity, inadequecy, hollowness and restlessness but he does not feel the need for commercial and money conscious civilization. He has no problem with the society but the contradictory impulses of reason and intuition, doubt and faith, religion and intuition, resistence and submission creates attention in him. One one hand he inherits from his grandfather love for womainsing, drinking and sensuality, on the other hand from his mother's side he gets the impulse to trust and to surrender. In between two emotions he becomes a Labyrinth. His contradictions make him rootless and gives him a feeling of confession :

> If only one knew — what one wanted. Or, may be, to know was what I wanted. To knows just that. No more. No less. This, then, was a labyrinth too, this going forward and backward and sideways of the mind (pp. 140).

Som Bhaskar passes through the arms of innumerable women but every time he finds a void with greater force. At every relationship he feels more discontented. Leela Sabnis attracts him more powerfully than others. For her reasons Som Bhaskar is dissatisfied. He is torn by the conflicts between faith and doubt. It is due to his Western-oriented materialistic education. He wants to believe, he tries to believe but he fails because he is helpless. Finally, he neglects his health, business and sanity. Through Som Bhaskar, Joshi explores the possibility of an equation between two cultures and self-realisation. In between the cultures of the two worlds Som Bhaskar suffers. He reveals that Western values do not provide peace, sublimity and self-fulfilment. Traditional Indian culture and values give us enlightment and greater force.

3

Aloneness and Rootlessness

The mankind as a whole faces today the problem of rootlessness which creates a sense of aloneness as Edmund Fuller remarks : man suffers not only from war, persecution, famine and run, but from inner problem.... a conviction of isolation, randomness, (and) meaninglessness in his way of existence.[1] The object poverty of the masses and the ever growing afluence of the newly rich, the fast changing values — all these make increasng and often disturbing on the individual and contribute in their own ways of his sense of alonenes in life. The treatment of this theme by Arun Joshi is no less interesting.

Joshi's characters are hopelessly lost. They find the lonely quarters in the dark recess of existence. Most of the characters are divided in their souls. They suffer from loneliness and thereby they feel the meaninglessness of life. The purpose in this chapter is to study Johsi's treatment of aloneness and rootlessness. The very first novel of Arun Joshi, *The Foreigner* has "a strange feeling of aloneness and aloofness, associated with the word, 'Foreigner' permeates the entire narrative and provides the necessarily texture and structure to the novel"[2].

> The protagonist Sindi Oberoi, who narrates the story, finds himself quite lonley in life. He is an existential character — rootless, restless and luckless in the world. He moves from London to Boston and to New Delhi all alone. He himself

---

1. *Man in Modern Fiction* (New York : Random House, 1958), p. 3.
2. Bhatnagar, O.P., *Arun Joshi's The Foregner* : *A Critism of East and West*, JIWE, 1, No. 2, 1973, pp. 13-14.

> admits that his life is 'alone in the darkness' (p.189).

In his life Sindi Oberoi has two lasting impressions while he was in London his association with Anna and Kathy taught him to practise detachment and non-involvement in human relationships. He comes to the final crisis in his life when he is in Boston. He develops an involvement for June, an attractive American girl. He is passionately chained, though for short lived, he fails in his determination not to get involved. He remains uninvolved to June's insistent love appeals and tries to drive her away into the arms of Babu Rao Khemka. After Khemka's involvement he helps him in his education and in his distress. Babu Rao Khemka also finds himself at sea all alone waiting for disaster.

Before the marriage of June and Khemka takes place, she is imprignated and Babu loses his balance. He tries to put an end to his life out of frustrations and failures at the examination. As a friend philosopher and guide Sindi says :

> When I had Come to gaining too detachment and had acted out of goodness. I had riven a man to his death (p. 174).

In his best efforts to maintain detachment Sindi Oberoi leaves Boston and takes up a job in New York. As a typical sympathiser he comes to know that June is with Babu's child and she needs his help and adivce. He expects June's death in case she tries for the abortion of the child but it is his absurd fate that he gets the news of Babu's death. The feeling of aloneness does not leave him even for a minute and he survives even after such unexpected turn of events.

The terrible consequences of his practice of detachment in America compels him to leave the country and to go to India. He does not know that what will happen to him in India. He decides within himself. He hopes to live in India, the life different from New York and Boston. He believes :

> Like many of my bread I believed erroneously that I could escape from a part of myself by hopping from one land mass to another (p. 176).

The new development in his life in India is not causal. He accepts a job in the firm of Babu Rao Khemka's father. He gets involved with Sheila in spite of his commitment to detachment. But finally he finds himself all alone, purturbed, brooding over his past life and anxious for the future. Here he admits his truth of life in the following lines :

> I saw myself as I had always been. An uprooted young man living in the latter half of the twentieth century, who had become detached from everything except himself (p. 195).

Sindi sees no purpose in life and he finds himself living without a purpose. Lying there in the bed in his apartment he wonders what he has made of his life. As a foreigner it makes no difference to him if he lives in India or in America or in Kenya. Everywhere it is the samething for him. He consoles his divided soul :

> Who knows where the road will lead? only to fool can say (p. 182).

In loneliness and despair Sindi is a self seeker and absurd man and an existential character. Though his experiences tell him not to be involved but he gets involved through love and goodness. It is simply chance that Sindi gets involved this way or that way but he wants to live the life of an Indian saint.

The Billy Biswas of Joshi's second novel, first of all appears to be a man of extraordinary obsessions but his deep roots in society and civilization is destroyed by his absurd meanderings. His quest is for values in a mad, bad, absurd world. He is attracted by the dark mysterious forces of the universe. Bilasia, the tribal girl drives him to the doors of death and he is seen with his existential visions. He is lost in his problems of identity. He meditates between New Delhi and Satpura Hills. His total alienation turns to be a rare spiritual regeneration. The New Delhi based civilization does not suit his temperament. He gets out with conscious choice to go to the Satpura Hills. He outright rejects his involvement with Meena Chatterjee and Rima Kaul and he begins to realise :

> It gradually dawned on me that a tremendous corrupting force was working on me. It was as though my soul were taking revenge on me for having denied it for so long that other thing that it had been clamouring for. "Here, you swine, if you have not the gust to break away from this filth, well, thin, I am going to wallow in it until it makes you sick" (p. 189).

Billy's aloneness with Meena and Rima gives him the central vision in his attachment with primitive Bilasia. He is on the verge of collapse in the company of Meena and Rima. He is unable to understand the relations. He is lost with the things around him but the pleasures of Satpura's Hills and the dream of his life all alone in the forest drives him into a fit of madness. His strange case of vision sounds strange to all of us. The woman he meets and those who notices him find him outside the reality and he seems to be a man constantly striving in his psyche for fulfilment of his dreams. His psychic interests him in the forest in sounds of drums and in the dance of the bhils. He doesnot find peace rather he finds materialism in his wife Meena :

> Her upbringing her ambitions, twenty years of contact with phoney society — all had ensured that she sould not have it. So more I tried to tell her what was coording me bringing me to the edge of despair so to speak, the more resentful she became (p. 187).

The landscapes, hills, valleys and the music of the drums attract him to take up the life of a lone primitive. When he enters the world of bhils and watches their druming and dance ceremonies, his unconscious mind gets some sorts of relief far from the madding crowd.

Billy all of a sudden disappears from the face of the eath into the sal forests of the Maikala Hills where he has taken previously with students on an expedition. For a year, the whole area is combed to trace him but he is not found. He is believed to be killed by the man-eater. Ten years after his disappearance, his friend Romi who is posted as a Collector in a district of the Central India, goes on a tour of interior villages, terribly ravaged by a draught. He is passing in his Jeep through the crowd of sufferings. At once he is taken aback by a man coming closer to him. The man addressess him :

> I say, old chap, you would not recognise me, would you? (p. 101).

To his great surprise, Romi sees Billy standing near him naked but for a loin cloth. He takes him to his Bungalow and spends the whole day and night in his company. What Billy tells him about his life after disappearance is the story of his aloneness alone.

Billy is drawn towards tribals life which he thinks answer to his quest for the purpose of his life. Even as a boy he is deeply concerned about the problem of his identity. When he is fourteen years old, he visits Bhubaneshwar and while watching sculptures he remarks :

> If any one had a clue to it (the spirit) it was only the adivasis who carried about their knowledge in silence locked behind their dark inscrutable faces (p. 124).

He also gets an opportunity to watch the dance of the tribals there which makes him feel 'a great shock of erotic engery'. He says to himself :

> Something has gone wrong with my life. This is where I belong. This is what I have always dreamt of (p. 125).

While he is teaching at Delhi University he takes his students for expedition to Central India, he is lured by the hills there. He likes aloneness of the dance forest. The whole hilly forest appears to call him to its primitive world. Thus, the son of a Supreme Court Justice becomes a tirbal, marries Bilasia and has a son from her. He likes this new life of a lone tribal :

> Nobody here is interested in the prices of foodgrains or new seeds on raods or elections and stuff like that. We talk of the super-natural, violent death, trees, earth, rain, dust storms, rivers,

> moods of the forest, animals, dance, singing. And we talk, I am afraid, a lot about woman and sex (p. 113).

Ratan Rathore, unlike Sindi and Billy, is a conscience torn man with a curious mixture of idealism and docility. He has a vague sense of values — a helpless self deceiver with a deep awareness of conflicts between life and living. It is not the story of Ratan Rathore but may be of every one of us.

The apprentice turns a fake, a corrupt official and an exhausted family man. His inside gets hollow and moth eaten. He looses his personality and identity, though he prepares an article on 'crisis of character' he shows a remarkable self awareness, exposing his oversubtlities, fads, preoccupations, self-deceptions, ego and boredom of the dark phase of his life, it gives a kind of complexity to his character. In whirpool of confusing values, contradictions, and enigmas he fails to comprehened the real meaning of his actions. His initial restlessness leads to apathy and we notice gradual change coming over to him. He passes through anger, remorse and intense suffering. Finally he writes out his confession and modifies it to justify his actions. Ratan Rathore has a different life to live than Sindi and Billy. His apprentice sense of the futility scalds him inwardly and leaves him exhausted that he tells his listeners most pathetically :

> So you see, my friend, here I am, a man without honour, a man without shame, perhaps a man of our times... How do I know life has purpose? Actually I do not. And, quite honestly mine is not the mind that can grasp such questions. But let me tell you something that a collegue of mine used to say. Life is a zero, he would say, and he would add, you can take nothing away from a zero... I have begun to see a flaw in the argument. You see, you can make it negative... Life might will be a zero, for all I know, but it seems to me that it need not be negative. And it becomes negative when you take of it your sense of shame, your honour (pp. 204-205).

Ratan Rathor is not an intellectual like Sindi or Billy but an ordinary man, who should appreciate the distinction between zero as negative. A zero as positive is indicative of the character's development. Ratan simply undergoes the strongest apprenticeship in the world. His vision of life and sensibility is guided by legends and tales of sin and expiation and those are purely Indian. Ratan Rathor has the same self introspection as Sindi has, but it has a compelling urgency for its concern. It has social background, but Sindi's individual outlook on life is far away from corruption and material gains. The social background of Billy is not an obstacle in his way. He rather chooses for the primitivism on his own accord. On the whole the convincing development of the protagonists does not limit the artistic scope or device in the fictional world of Arun Joshi.

In Joshi's Sindi, the original sense of insecurity, isolation and forced detachment gives him meaning in the larger context of life. Kamala Markanday also projects the identity problem in *The Nowhere Man*, she probes deeper into human motivations and tries to depict the existential predicament of rootlessness. Her Srinivas longs to belong to a "wider citizenship", but Vasantha his wife, a typical Indian wife, refuses to assimlate the culture of her adopted land. At the sudden death of his younger son first and Vasantha later, Srinivas feels no meaning in life. He is lost in the new loneliness. His leprosy is symptomatic of his physical and emotional isolation. He is considered and condemned as an 'unwanted man', 'an intruder', an alien, and labelled as a leper, to be 'obstracized further.'[3] Srinivas is a rootlesss creature like Sindi and Mohan Biswas.

The loss of roots in Indian culture imples deritualisation and eventually loss of its content. The acquisition of an unassimilated alien, culture renders it further meaningless. Such a situation definds the ambivalence of the East Indian personality and yields place to a pragmatic concern for the immediate contingencies of existence. The restlessness in Joshi's novels is a historical recorder

---

3. Markanday Kamla : *The Nowhere Man*, p. 193.

of the cultural scene. The Indian mind is characterised by a plasticity and resilence which appear strange and irrational to the West. The displaced Indian next finds himself in a precarious and an uncertain situation, the worst fear of being left behind. This thesis Joshi carries in his fictional works. Joshi's characters are different from Rajan's Krishna, or Sahgal's Sanad Shivpal or even from Kamla Markanday's Srinivas or Raja Rao's Ramaswamy. They all, in way or another, face Jamesean dilemma of double cultures impringing upon the self. His characters are more modern beings, much less complete, much less authentic. Though they are Indian in essence, they come closer to Kafka's heroes or camus outsiders. Sindi's rootlessness is a result of the cumulative forces, his inter-racial parentage, his inter-culture orientation and above all, his personal experiences in abroad and in India. His a problem of existence. He has never been loved nor can be ever loved in the real sense. His Billy Biswas is a transformed Sindi Oberoi, who casts off his urban civilization and goes to the forest. The life of his Ratan Rathore is a journey from innocence to experience and also from self-love to self-remorse. In a way Som Bhaskar in *The Last Labyrinth* is similar to Billy Biswas because he too is in search of something. Joshi says :

> Yes, there is similarity between the two. The faceless God is prominent in Billy Biswas inner thoughts. One finds the same facelessness in Som Bhaskar.[4]

In Joshi the heroes have progressed from alienation to existential affirmation. *The Last Labyrinth* is only exception. Joshi confirms it in a letter to V. Gopal Reddy dated Jan. 8, 1981, alienation of my novels with I have written so far ultimately leads them back to community. I realised that in my latest novel *The Last Labyrinth* for the first time it does not happen.[5] The novel ends with Som making a suicidal attempt by putting the revolver casually to his

4. Banerjee Purabi, *A Winner's Secrets* : An Interview with Purabi Banerjee, *The Sunday Statesman,* 27 Feb. 1983.
5. Reply to V. Gopal Reddy, dated Jan. 8, 1981.

temple. As he tries to kill himself, he is stopped by Gita who shakes him gently as though rousing a man from sleep (p. 224). While Sindi in *The Foreigner* depends on his philosophy of non-involvement, Ratan in *The Apprentice* holds on to his careerism. Sindi slowly learns that real detachment lies in involvement. In the same manner Ratan's sense of alienation makes him understand that a combinaton of humanism and religion can be the saving grace of mankind steeped in corruption. The cause of alienation and inner emptiness of Ratan is neither the rootlessness of Sindi nor the unusual urge of Billy. He also feels that one cannot live for onself because no human act is performed in isolation and without consequence. Hence, out of an acute sense of alienation and a quest to understand the meaning of life, he takes up apprenticeship. At a deeper level, *The Foreigner* can be viewed as an attempt to seek man's perennial dilemmas. In his eagerness to find out the meaning of life he lives "in a strange world of intense pleasure and almost equally intense plan" (p. 82). His sufferings are manifestation of a spiritual crisis which all sensitive people have to face today. He wants peace, a capacity to love and the courage to live "without desire and attachment" (p. 138). All his attempts in this regard, however, fizzle out "like an ill-packed cracker" (p. 139). In this chapter I have tried to show the sense of aloneness and rootlessness of man which has threatened the existence today. The characters of Joshi are mouthpieces of this emotional problem. The condition in India, though not so alarming as in the Western world, have started to take a dismal turn. The moral confusion of modern Indians who live on an *ad-hoc* basis, adopting a dual code of behaviour, has been discussed. The novelist has tried to project the crisis through the character's experiences in the modern civilization and the impact of this emotional problem on the individual. Joshi's characters are trapped in their own loneliness and rootlessness.

His herores are misfit and they find themselves lonely and rootless in the world they have to live in and face pathlessness and meaninglessness. To escape this feeling, his protagonists make relentless efforts to find out meaning in life. In this effort they get sympathetic attachment or involvement. Most of them are haunted by a sense of futility. They are ready to encounter whatever comes in the way.

✪

4

Mixing Fantasy and Reality

The artist's imagination transforms the material which is drawn from real life, fashions and facts. Truly speaking situation plays a significant part in the making of art or artistic creations. Imagination as well as reality is the basis of every realist artist. The artist transforms the familiar raw materials with the help of his creative imagination into artistic pictures. These pictures appear different from objects known to us. In fiction, fantasy alone disregards the principle that literature should present not the possible, but the probable as it combines action, characters or setting under ordinary conditions or in the normal course of events. As Jane Eklund Ball observes "the term fantasy applies to any work of literature or art in which imagination is freed from the restraints of natural law — that is, from the limitations of everyday reality."[1]

Though fantasy deals with unreal inventions of supersensory perceptions and irrational associations. Fantasy can also try on all moods and can follow a variety of conventions. It can show our suppressed terror, but it cannot make us forget the unpleasant things or circumstances. It generally discovers the truths that lie under the surface of life. Thus, it is the source of deepest truths about the inner life. It has two aspects hidden — high seriousness and great entertaining quality. So it appeals to wide range of readers. On the one hand, it satirizes social evils, on the other hand, it gives the mind welcome relief from the unpleasant and relieves the mental tensions caused by individual sense of frustration.

---

1. Ball Eklund Jane, *The Range of Literature* : Fiction (Boston, Houghton Mifflin), p. 217.

The modern fantasy is inspired by Freudian psychology which also seems to give it a new lease of life. The neurotic acts of characters are the result of these fantasies which involves subconscious and unconscious urges, but these fantasies have roots in real life whichever comprehensible in relation to reality. It is the normal and the fantastic which attracts us in Kafka's stories and novels. His characters have the tendency to be unknown, unnatural and fantastic. Like Kafka, Arun Joshi tries to present psychic imbalances and impulsive actions of his characters. He avoids realistic portraiture leaving out the details of their social world. His protagonists are individualistic and self-centered. All of them are highly educated — their conduct is incompatible with the natural laws of every day reality. Violation of common cord of life or social life is not uncommon to them. Alienated from the society, they try to work out for their own identity and they work on their own choice. They are not free from the urges of their sub-conscious self. The psychic imbalances of Sindi Oberoi in *The Foreigner* pushes him into unprecedented relationships and keeps him rootless as a foreigner till the last. Billy Biswas in *The Strange Case of Billy Biswas* is pushed by "a great force, upkraft, a primitive force" of his unconscious self and disregards the respectability of his high middle class society. He seeks his roots in the company of primitive tribals. It results into anguish to his family and his tragic end. Ratan Rathor, in *The Apprentice* is trapped by his irrational environment. He suffers to extricate his soul. Som Bhaskar in *The Last Labyrinth* is driven by undefined hungers of his inner self while he wants to possess a woman with feverish intensity. In this way the fantasy has its basis in the narratives of Arun Joshi as the irrational actions of his heroes. *The Foreigner* is written from protagonist narrators point of view and the novel has descriptions of experiences of the hero Sindi Oberoi as a student of Mechanical Engineering in the American University in Boston and in the later part of his life as an employee in the firm of Khemka, a wealthy industrialist in Delhi. After the first chapter which deals with the death of Babu in car accident in Boston and its emotional impact on Sindi and June. The narrative follows flash ahead and flash back technique to unfold incidents of the story. While Sindi evades Sheila's queries, he feels haunted by Babu's ghost and recapitulates events in Boston in which these three (Sindi, Babu and June) were involved. Thus, the experiences of America are recounted in flashback. The novelist maintains suspense connected with the life of the hero, Sindi Oberoi. The novelist gives a realistic description of the self-consciousness and excitements of new comers to America. Babu, there in America turns into a split personality. He loves to enjoy the free life in America. He tells Sindi :

> I think it is a wonderful country. I would never go back to India if I had the choice (p. 90).

He further adds :

> Sometimes I wish I had been born in America. Not that I have anything against India but there is nothing to beat America (p. 91).

He, however, comes of an orthodox Hindu Family and is unable to divest himself of its traditional ethical values in making adjustment with American life. He has deep respect for his father who has made him to visit America for educational purposes. He has no courage to annoy him. In such divided state of mind he is neither able to devote himself to his studies nor capable of enjoying American life. June assesses his position in the following way :

> This father of his since to be an awful bully. I am sure things would be much simpler if he were not always there in the background, sending those long summons and to telling him what's wrong with him and how he should convey himself (p. 123).

Because of his moral inhibitions and traditional background Babu fails in his relation with June that drives both of them to the tragic end. In June Blyth he looks for virginal purity of an ideal Indian girl. He does understand "that codes of morality differ from country to country (p. 55). He avoids physical relations with her as she admits :

> I wish to God I know. I just don't know. Initially, I thought he just wanted me physically. When he didn't make any advances I told him he could have me whenever he felt like that. He said he did't want to do it until after the wedding (p. 158).

She does not simply want Babu's love but something more than that. She finds whole thing confused. We see her longing hearts in her following assertion :

> It would have been so much easier if he had just wanted my body. In five minutes it is over. A woman can see the look of satisfaction and gratitude and even feel gratified in return. But here it is just one long drawn out agony. Each minute is loaded with the throbbing of a climax which never comes (p. 159).

She further writes to Sindi :

> I am utterly at a loss what to do. In such matters I used to do what you told me but you are not here and I suppose you are not interested. Any way, it is good to have at least got it out of my system (p. 160).

C.N. Srinath points out that from *The Foreigner* to *The Strange Case of Billy Biswas* there is a movement from the almost contemplative world of Sindi to the dynamic, vital and active world of Billy (Bimal Biswas).[2]

M. Asnani is of the opinion that novel is the story of horror, suspense, mystery and romance. It presents a clash between 'nature' and art. The hollow 'civilized' life acts as a pivot for the theme of alienation to revolve.

D.R. Sharma points out that when Billy discovers that the prevailing social order is difficult to redesign, he opts out for the

---

2. C.N. Srinath, *The Fiction of Arun Joshi, The literary criterion,* 12, Nos. 2-3, p. 119.

tribal world which operates in a simpler and clearer manner. Hence, Billy can be called an Indian Huck Finn, or a Henderson whom mere material prosperity cannot distract from the pursuit of abiding values.[3] Billy feels alienated because he craves for a full individuality unfettered by the state convention of society.

Joshi has exploited the resourceful technique of the first person narration in this novel more than in his two other novels. The story is related partly in the first person by Billy himself partly gathering through other characters and mostly summarized by the narrator. A long continuous account would not have been interesting; but it would not have revealed the multiple facts of truth. This shift in the point of view helps Joshi to probe the mind of the protagonist in dispassionate and objective vein. It enables the dramatic presentation of the complex characters of Billy whose values are profoundly human and yet aspiring after something beyond the human. To some extent the story of the novel is narrated through Ramesh Sahai, the District Collector and also one time fellow student of Billy Biswas abroad.

Billy's recognition of other civilizations and other sets of value systems is at the root of his inner anguish and quest for selfhood. His sense of alienation takes him into another world, a primitive society, which is not governed by artificial codes of behavior even Ramesh Sahai ceases to understand Billy.

Billy had only two choices before him. He could either follow the call of primitivism, whatever the cost, or be condemned to total decay. He is very much averse to the corruption prevalent in the contemporary society and more so in the urban elite in India :

> I don't think all city societies are as shallow as ours. I am of course, talking mainly of the so called upper class. I didn't really get to know the others. I don't think I have ever met a more

3. Sharma D.R., *The Fictional World of Arun Joshi,* The Indian Pen, 41, Nos. 9-10.

> pompous, a more mixed up lot of people. Artistically they were dry as dust. Intellectually they could no better than mechanically mouth ideas that the West abandoned a generation ago. Their ideas of romance was to go and see an American movie or go to out of those wretched restaurants and dance with their wives to a thirty year old tune (p. 179).

Romi is the only link of civilization for Billy. He has all the admiration and sympathy for Billy. He strives to protect him from the recalling arms of civilization. In the struggle that follows, modern civilization proves itself to be the stronger and Billy can no longer enjoy his privacy. The effort to capture him leads to final catastrophe. Billy dies of bullet wounds. Only his ashes reach the civilized world from which Billy opted out.

Towards the end Romi almost identifies herself with Billy's concern. When the police force is mobilized to capture Billy, the collector himself feels trapped :

> I felt now that it was not merely Billy Biswas but Billy and I together who were being hunted down (p. 208).

Thus *The Strange Case of Billy Biswas* has been disposed of in the only manner that a humdrum society does with its rebels, its seers, and its true lovers. While the civilized world destroys him, the tribal world seeks to perpetuate the memory of the man-god by building him a shrine. Here fantasy and reality both comes closer. On one side fantasy takes the readers to enjoy the things in the civilized society, on the other hand the reality makes it a tale of utmost importance. Both the situations give it a peculiar insight.

In *The Apprentice,* although Ratan Rathor is well settled in life, he cannot feel a sense of satisfaction because he holds his career dear and sacrifices the principles that have guided him all the while. In spite of all the material comforts available to him, discontentment has become a way of life for Ratan. He finds himself deeply lost in the corrupt atmosphere. For the sake of confirmation and promotion, Ratan is forced to marry a girl related to the superintendent, though he is not primarily interested. It doesn't take much time for him to realize that world runs on deals. In fact his own marriage is a deal for his career :

> If men forget how to make deals the world would come to a stop. It would lose its propelling power. Men would not know what to do with themselves. It is not the atom or the Sun or God or sex that lies at the heart of the universe : it is deals. DEALS..... They are simply there, like air (p. 51).

In the process of these strange bargains with the world Ratan becomes a hypocrite. His hypocrisy fetches him a car, a bungalow, and a good place in society at the cost of his peace of mind. Thus, his conscience degenerates totally and suffers a 'crisis of character.' In short he becomes a whore in the pursuit of his career and ends up ultimately by accepting a bribe when he least needs money. At every stage he puts up an initial resistance only to discover the futility of his efforts like so many others of his kind in the contemporary society. He leads a frustrated and exhausted family life. The more money he accumulates, the more dissatisfied he is. A strange fear of death haunts him all the time. He feels restless.

When the brigadier is on the brink of madness in a military hospital, Ratan feels that some priceless essence that he has known and recognized for forty years, has vanished. It is second time in his life that he has felt the pain of another as his own, the first being the time when his father was shot :

> And standing there by the glass window I felt as though it was not the Brigadier but I who was rocking through some dark dungeons of the world (p. 103).

At first Ratan is mentally resolved to see his friend. He writes his confession, but modify it instantly and tries to justify his act by convincing himself of his 'innocence' and finally pockets the confession letter forever. Now his main concern is to get out of this mess he had made. The Brigadier could not, however, wait for his confession and he kills himself.

Ratan realizes that there is no end to human vanity, or, for that matter, to human stupidity. The dead Brigadier's vision trails him wherever he goes. Ratan is filled with an endless torment of fear. He realizes the gravity of his sin. At last his alert consciousness alienates him from the degenerated society :

> Twenty years and nothing gained. An empty life time. What I had learned? Pushing files? Manoeuvring? At forty five all that I knew was to manoeuvres. A trickster, that was what I have let make me. Did I know the meaning of honour, friendship. Did I ever know it? Would I ever know it again? (p. 139).

Ratan realizes that his life had been a great waste. He is not sure of what precisely corrupted the atmosphere of the society. He feels that the need for doing something for changing the prevailing situation. But he is full of doubts about the way to read the society of this corruption. He finally realizes that one cannot live for oneself because no human act is performed in isolation and without consequence. Therefore, each act should be performed in isolation and without consequence. Therefore, each act should be performed with a sense of alienation and a quest to understand the meaning of life. He undergoes the sternest apprenticeship in the world. He has lost self and felt the anguish of loss. He takes existential decision for his integrity.

Like *The Foreigner,* Joshi's fourth novel *The Last Labyrinth* is also written from the protagonist narrator's point of view. The hero, Som Bhaskar, is a millionaire industrialist, relates in flashback the events involving him and another man's woman for whom he lusts with feverish intensity and for whose possession he risks his business and life. For him, his relentless pursuit of this woman, which becomes the centre of his entire existence, assures the dimensions of his quest for the greatest of all mysteries the last labyrinth *i.e.,* death.

Joshi's novels read like a fantasy because of intriguing juxtaposition of the sensual and the spiritual, weird locals, a crumbling haveli, labyrinth within labyrinth of lanes, housing dancing girls and ascetics, a Don-Juan like hero with undefined hungers.

Generally Joshi begins his novels like plausible pieces of reality but soon exaggerates them to the point of fantasy. Not only this he introduces a set of irrational associations typical of a powerful fantasy. Due to this fusion of fantasy and reality, his stories keep the eagerness of the readers on tiptoe and maintain readers' undivided interest in the novel to the end.

5

Predicament and Meaninglessness

The predicament and meaninglessness of modern man has been delineated by certain recent Indian novelists in English. In the works of Joshi we see that how man has lost his spiritual moorings. All the heroes of Joshi are "men engaged in the meaning of life." In all his works Josh, the novelist tries to sketch the pen picture of the urbanized and industrialised modern civilization along with its dehumanising impact on the individual who is ever eager to find out the meaning of all life and existence. In spite of the frequently repeated calls for 'cnracinement' in literature for the individual talent to be rooted in the traditions of a particular culture, the strength of modern literary imagination lies in its evocation of the individual's predicament in terms of alienation or exile or quest for identity. In the third world literature we find the theme of individuals predicament in the form of rootlessness and crisis of identity. But my concern in this chapter is to examine the human predicament and meaninglessness in the novels of Arun Joshi.

The Foreigner explores the individual's anguished consciousness of being isolated from the whole apparatus of convention and ritual of society. It examines the problem of isolation and involvement and man's despair at being unable to find a meaning in existence. The protagonist of the novel, Sindi Oberoi is irritated and embarrassed to find himself in the predicament of an outsider. He is an orphan. The fluidity of his background emphasises his metaphysical alienation. A queer persons, Sindi clearly does not belong. He is a man drifting aimlessly on the surface of life without an anchor to cling. Rootless as he is, Sindi's life takes him to London, Boston and New Delhi. He had his education in London where he meets Anna a minor artist separated from her husband., He has an affair with this soho artist who yearns neither for him nor anybody but for her lost youth. Later he is deeply involved with Kathy, an English house wife, who leaves Sindi after carrying on with him for a few weeks and goes back to her husband because she thought marriage was sacred and had to be maintained at all costs. The appalling living conditions of Muthu's large family make Sindi aware of the accumulated despair of their weary lives. Sindi is shocked to his very depths when Muthu gives an expression to the misery of his life.

> But it becomes difficult to remain calm when you find so many children going hungry most of the time... I wouldn't worry so much if I could at least be sure of food for these people (p. 225).

Sindi is deeply touched by the squalor of the place and the wretchedness of Muthu's lot. Earlier he had sympathized with the labourers and indicated Mr. Khemka for exploiting his workers :

> It is you who have swindled those miserable wretches in rags who push carts on your streets and die at twenty five. It is you who have been telling lies and fabricating documents just so that you could air-condition this ostentatious house and throw gigantic parties for the horde of jackals who masquerade as your friends (p. 226).

The poverty, the deprivation and the helplessness of the workers make Sindi take cudgels for them. He is shocked to find the employees in mortal dread of Sheila and Mr. Khemka.

Sindi Oberoi, the main character in the novel *The Foreigner*, compares himself with a tree without roots. He feels himself an orphan and a stranger everywhere : in Boston, in Kenya where he was born, in London where he was educated, and in India, the land of his ancestors, where he has come back only because it is as good a place to forget himself as any other. His estrangement is explained by his fate as an orphan change of places, and by many other things. It creates spiritual depression in his soul;

everything in the world is alien to him, but he cannot get rid of his own self.

Sindi pessimistic attitude is aggravated by the fact that he does not have faith in anything : neither in God, nor in the motherland, nor in revolution nor in love. He does not have any ideals. It is possible to judge his distrust in historical progress by the conversation between him and the tax-collector, Ghosh, who is presented as a revolutionary by the author :

> The revolution may come, I (Sindi-E.K.) said, And you know what will happen when it does. You will be shot. I will be shot.The rest will remain unchanged. The charlatans you wish to destroy will just turn around and put on another mask. A few individuals don't matter. What is important is that the proletariat will rule.
>
> * * * *
>
> The proletariat you speak of will most likely be coralled into communes and driven like slaves.
>
> * * * *
>
> That may be in beginning. Said the income tax man, Sacrifice is inevitable in a revolution. That is precisely where you are wrong. There is never a beginning. Nor is there an end. There is no end to suffering, no end to the struggle between good or evil (pp. 40-41).

The novel starts as a standard detective with the verification of a corpse. In a motor car accident the student Babu Rao, the son of a factory owner, dies. In his pocket the photograph of a girl June is found. The girl was a acquaintance of Sindi, who informs her about Babu's death. From this place, the spindle of the thematic thread unfolds into the past. Sindi is not capable of sincerity and deep feelings. Egoism of his nature is invincible. He saw for the first time an American girl June, a beautiful blonde with light blue eyes, in one of the balls of International Students Association. Later she, by coincidence, gave him a lift in such a way as their acquaintance began, and developed into love on the part of June. Sindi is also infatuated by Shiela, Babu Rao's sister. As it is obvious from his internal monologue, Sindi himself is well aware of it :

> And at times I (Sindi-E.K.) made love to her (June E.K.) not because I described her but because I wanted to make sure that she still loved me what made matters worst was that nearly everything we met June told me that she loved me. This only aggravated the burden of my guilt (84).

Although Sindi continues to meet June, he does not object against Babu Rao's courting her. When Babu comes to know that June loves Sindi, he prefers to disappear from life. After the news of his death, June, who is carrying a child from him, decides in despair to undergo an abortion in hospital and during the operation she dies. It is too late for Sindi to realize that he is guilty of the death of both, and he seized by belated repentance :

> Wouldn't Babu still be living if I have not surrendered my body to June that night we went for a ride?... And if Babu had not killed himself June would still be living (p. 196).

After such an unexpected, almost simultaneous death of two young people. Sindi goes away to India and tries to fill up the spiritual vacuum by studies of Indian philosophy, but all in vain :

> You don't understand, Sheila said, you don't understand India and you don't understand Indian traditions (p. 56).

In this narrative, the Indian comprehension of life is diluted and there are no descriptions of national customs. There is also an absence of historical background in the novel. The author tries to convey only the external impulses of man. But there is attempt to discuss some principles of Indian philosophy in the spirit of existentialism. It is not by chance that in one of the reviews published in the magazine Indian writing. Today, The literary critic R.P. Rama writes :

> There are moments when Arun Joshi's handling of ideas appear phoney : Indian philosophy grafted an experience which is the usual stuff of extential literature.[1]

It is true that some critics, including Khushwant Singh, have put in the press complimentary reviews of Arun Joshi's novel, foretelling him a big future. Experiencing the direct influence of the French writer, Arun Joshi has followed him (camus) and has created works about the aimless existence of a man who is indifferent to everything and alien to everybody, works which are rather a brilliant illustration of the Indian variety of existentialism.

Billy, of *The Strange Case of Billy Biswas*, like Sindi, is also in search of human world of emotional fullness — a world of meaningful relatedness, which can be find either in white America or in the upper class Indian society. Billy is of the view that something has gone wrong with the whole world because initially it was :

> What need would there be of Psychiatrists, research foundations, learned societies, great scholars, Scientists, ministerial advisers, ambassadors, generals, had the world not initially been hung on this peg of money (p. 97).

He admires the Swedish girl Tulla for her ability to treat money for what it is worth : a whole lot of paper. Billy's withdrawal from the world is in the nature of a reflex action, he withdraws in order to preserve himself from the mendacity around him which had also begun to make inroad into his character. Long before his physical disappearance into the Saal forests of the Maikala Hills, he had ceased to belong to the world. Billy, in a way, is driven out by the shallowness of civilization and by the failure of his marriage which might have been saved if :

---

1. R.P. Rama, *Indo-Anglian Review, Arun Joshi's The Foreigner,* Indian writing Today (July-September 1970) Vol. IV, No. 3, p. 167.

> Meena had possessed a rare degree of empathy or even a sufficient idea of human suffering but her upbringing, her ambitions, twenty years of contact with a phoney society — all had ensured that she could not have it (p. 185).

Though Billy withdraws from the humdrum world, he does not withdraw from the world of love and pain, or from the world of senserality and sensitiveness and this he finds in the Saal forests, among the aboriginals, in his relationship with Bilasia who reflects the primitive force which Tulla had long ago sensed in Billy. When he meets Bilasia, Billy feels :

> I don't believe I had ever felt towards any other woman what I felt towards Bilasia that night. And I don't think I shall ever feel it again, even towards Bilasia. I t was that passing moment that rarely comes in a man's life, when he feels that he has suddenly discovered that bit of himself that he has searched for all his life and without which his life is nothing more than the poor reflection of a million others.
>
> * * * *
>
> She seemed like another vision, elusive as a gust of passing wind. But, then, the truest perceptions of life, for me at least have always proved to be the most elusive and the most short-lived. The essence of life, it seems to me can be communicated only in the language of visions, and what vision has lasted a period even as short as a man's life (p. 142).

It is in this life that Billy finds fulfilment and identification and the essence of human existence. Later, when he discloses his identity there is no underlying motive to return to the civilized world. Only a desire to prevent bloodshed. Billy has to pay with his life for this magnanimous gesture, the

> Only manner that a humdrum society knows of disposing its rebels, its seers, its true lovers, all

> those who dare to step out of its stiffing confines (p. 240).

While civilized world destroys him the tribal world seeks to perpetuate the memory of the man-god by building him a shrine.

Ratan Rathor in *The Apprentice* takes almost a lifetime to reject the "petrified and frozen" world of civilization for he is the child of a double inheritance : the patriotic and courageous world of his father is matched by the worldly wisdom of his mother who tells him :

> It was not patriotism but money... that brought respect and bought security. Money made friends. Money succeeded where all else failed. There were many laws... but money was a law unto itself (p. 20).

Ratan aquires these things by learning to keep up appearances and by discarding the world of ordinary decency and friendships. He succumbs totally to the needs of his job and accepts a bribe along with security and promotion. In short he becomes a whore in the pursuit of his career and ends up ultimately by accepting a bribe when he least needs money. At every stage he puts up an initial resistance only to discover the futility of his effort like so many others of his kind for no one seemed sure whether :

> what was right was practicable. That was where the rub lay. In the practicability of things. That was where I saw the best of them buckle. Because very often the best did not have the daring or the greed of the charlatans.Thus the charlatans won. And when they saw the charlatans winning the best became even less sure of themselves. And at times they turned charlatans (p. 64).

In the end Ratan has to confess even in order to save his friend the Brigadier. And when he visits a temple in order to draw courage from the world of religion, he discovers that even religion is not free from corruption and no succour can be drawn from here. Ratan Rathor is shaken out of his moral inertia only by the faceless head of the dead Brigadier and the outspokenness of Himmat Singh who in his pitiless way contrasts their two lives : "My father he said, was a revolutionary, his mother a whore" (p. 144). Though their lives were empty and barren yet there was a difference, he was evengoing the loss of his mother's honour, while Ratan was selling himself. Even if life lacked a purpose, it need not lack a sense of satisfaction. Ratan realises that life may well be a zero, but it need be negative. It is now that he learns the lesson of humility :

> I never enter the temple. I can concerned with what goes on in there. I stand at the doorstep and I fold my hands, my hands smelling of leather and I say things. Be good, I tell myself. Be good. Be decent. Be of use (p. 148).

And being of use means doing the best one can — "without vanity, without expectations and also without cleverness." Thus, Joshi's foreigners turn inwards to resolve their sense of futility, to become integrated in some degree and to find a meaning in life, however, limited.

Ratan finds himself a misfit in the modern world. All his education and intelligence did not help him. He had to abdicate his true self to fit in the corrupt society and eke out a living. He is alienated from his true self and his ideals. In his feverish pursuit of careerism, he submits himself to all sorts of corruption that the modern world offers. In spite of all the material comforts available to him, discontentment becomes a way of life. He leads a frustrated and exhausted family life. His corrupt deal at the end costs the life of the Brigadier, his closest friend. He realises the gravity of his sin. At last his alert consciousness alienates him from the degenerated society. Ratan himself describes his own aberrations with a sense of self-awareness and objectivity :

> Twenty years and nothing gained. An empty lifetime. What had I learned? Pushing files? manoeuvring? At fortyfive all that I knew was to manoeuvre. A trickster, that was what I had felt life make of me. Did I know the meaning of

> honour, friendship? Did I ever know it? Would I ever know it again? (p. 139).

He learns the lessons of humility. He seeks his fulfilment in this symbolic act. He earnestly pleads with the young that there is nothing wrong to make a second start :

> One must try and not lose heart, not yield, at any cost to despair (p. 149).

The whole business of living in a muddle confuses him all the more and Ratan fails to differentiate between right and wrong. He lurks :

> The feeling generated in me a great confusion. What had I done, what had I done which I should not have done? What was right, what was wrong? What was the measure for doing things or not doing them? Where were the dividing lines : between success and failure, loyalty and betrayal, love and hate? (p. 140).

The highly sophisticated civilization has produced an average typical dilemma for Ratan. With a troubled conscience Ratan goes from place to place without finding any peace or solace. He confesses to Himmat Singh :

> That is a terrible sensation... the realisation that one's life has been a total waste, a great mistake; without purpose, without results. There are many sorrows in the world, but there is nothing in the three worlds to match the sorrow of a wasted life All else, thoughts of revenge, of pleasure, of pain, pale before it, are made pointless... I did not yet know what had happened to me but my life had been a great, great waste (pp. 72-73).

The sense of alienation in Ratan Rathor makes him understand that a combination of humanism and religion can be the saving grace of mankind steeped in corruption.

Arun Joshi's recent novel *The Last Labyrinth* also aims at delineating the human predicament. It probes into the turbulent inner world of an industrialist, Som Bhaskar who becomes a millionaire at the age of thirty. The novel plunges into a haunting world of life, love, God and Death, the greatest of all mysteries — "the last labyrinth." The novel raises some pertinent questions about life and its meaning and tries to unravel the still unresolved mysteries of God and Death.

In the very beginning of the novel Som realises that he has "become a nuisance" and he has been fooling around "like a clown performing before a looking glass." A great roaring hollowness inside his soul and "the boredom and the fed-up-ness" tormented him constantly resulting from his variegated experiences. He becomes "a worn-out weary man incapable of spontaneous felling" at the age of thirty-five. In his own estimation, he is "wondering, curious, analysing, correlating [but] getting nowhere." Once he says to Anuradha :

> I'll tell you what is wrong...I am dislocated. My mind is out of focus. There is something sitting right in front of me and I cannot see it (p. 107).

The root cause of Som's problems is that he is relentlessly chased by undefined hungers. He is always haunted by mysterious voices :

> ...audible only to my ears, a grey cry threshed the night air : I want. I want. I want. Through the light of my days and the blackness of my nights and the disquite of those sleepless hours...I had sung the same strident song : I want. I want. I want. I want (p. 11).

Being in possession of an object, a business enterprise and a woman named Anuradha of indeterminate age and origin, tall, handsome and tender he tries to quench his ravaging desires. His desires, however, know, no satisfaction. He remembers :

> ...for many years now, I have had this awful feeling that I wanted something. But the sad thing was it did not make the slightest difference when I managed to get what I had wanted. My hunger was just as bad as ever....Later it became more confused... A world spinning all by itself (p. 189).

Anuradha, who knew Som so well, explains the reasons of his unhappiness and dissatisfaction. She says :

> You don't want me. You don't know what you want. You don't know what is wrong and you don't know what you want (p. 106).

Leela Sabnis thinks that his troubles originate from his habit of "always playing games with the world." She bluntly tells him :

> You are lonely on the one hand. on the other, you have built a shell around yourself...you are bored, bored stiff in your little shell. That is the long and the short of it (p. 80).

As a consequence of his grim experience in life, Som develops "a new loathing for the squalid world." He is disgusted with people and himself. He maintains :

> It is the voids of the world, more than its objects, that bother me. The voids and the empty spaces, within and without (p. 47).

And on Manikarnika in Banaras he finds

> Voids with a bang. Both within and without... voids all (p. 48).

To know the meaning of life Som is urged on by a kin desire. But he fails to make any headway in this regard. The world remains to him "a mysterious world, as pretentious and meaningless as the holy bulls of Banaras." He tries his best to have a peep into its mystery. His interest in its secrets is genuine. As he himself says :

> Nothing had interested me more than the secrets of the universe (p. 129).

He further says :

> Why should there be this turn to evolution? Why should man be equipped, burdened with this strange...this strange sensibility, or urge or drive? Is it by chance? or, is there a meaning to it (p. 131).

The questions about life and death continue to haunt him throughout his life. "And always in various shades of coherence," he confides,

> The spoken or unspoken question, like a vulture, circled the corps of my life; what is lay in the last labyrinth? (p. 122).

Som would also like to know where one went after this life :

> Was this it, then? The terminus? The last of the labyrinth? A tobacco-stained house; a register with my father's signature; a temple on a hill; flags in the wind; a deaf-mute priestess; hints of miracle? was it this that I had wanted all my life? (p. 211).

Som's search for life's secrets becomes hopelessly complicated because of his yearning to have the best of both of worlds — the world of matter and of spirit. He maintains :

> What I needed, perhaps, was something, somebody, somewhere in which the two worlds combined (p. 82).

Such wishes are not normally granted and one is in for frustration and disillusionment. Som also suffers in life, as his friend K. puts it, on account of his proneness to "romanticizing...blowing things larger than life." Speaking of the unfortunate situation he is trapped in, Som himself observes :

> But there was always this bit of me, a large bit somewhere between the head and the chest, just idling about like a stationary engine, getting involved with nothing. It made me feel as though I was asleep. This was no joke. In fact it was one of the weirdest things to happen to anybody... (pp. 109-10).

At a deeper level, *The Foreigner* can be viewed as an attempt to plumb man's parennial dilemmas. It is about things that Sindi wants — the courage to be and the capacity to love. His alienation is of the soul and not of geography. As he himself confides, his "foreignness" lies "within" him and drives him from crisis to crisis rendering it difficult for him to leave "himself" behind wherever he goes. Right from the beginning, he is oppressed by a desire to find "the meaning of life." He himself wants to do something meaningful. His entire life is geared around his quest for permanence in life. He urges with himself on the meaning of life and its affairs.

In his eagerness to find out the meaning of life, Sindi lives "in a strange world of intense pleasure and almost equally intense pain." But he fails to make a satisfactory progress and, as he himself tells us, his twenty-five years are largely wasted in search of wrong things in wrong places. His soul becomes a battlefield where the child and the adult warred unceasingly.

The pathlessness of the road to New York reminds Sindi of his own pathlessness. He also remembers the lines, from a popular song which run :

> Who knows where the road will lead only a fool
> can say.

He becomes conscious of the fact that for no less than twenty years he "had moved whichever way life had led" him. He compares his meaningless existence to that of "an idiot without a keeper. Fully convinced of the abominable absurdity of the world" and "tired of living", he even contemplates suicide. He becomes consequently

> Cynical and exhausted, grown old before (his)
> time, weary with his own loneliness (p. 82).

Sindi wants to leave America to escape a bit of himself "that appeared the most decayed." Nigeria or India is the choice and the flip of the coin decides in favour of India. He comes to India hoping that it will provide him "a place to anchor on this lonely planet," but his hopes are belied. He finds India no better than America : "In truth it had only been a change of theatre from America; the show had remained unchanged."[2] He only has to

---

2. *Ibid.*, p. 207.

face here a different set of people with a different set of varieties and different ways of squeezing happiness out of a mad world."[3] He is appalled by "the stagnant deadness" of the Indian scene dominated by people like Mr. Khemka, "man of the world...owner of a growing empire."

Sindi feels himself stranger in India to both the corrupt rich man and the half-naked struggling labourer. The common people, he finds, "have the benefit of their delusions, which protect them from the lonely meaninglessness" of life. But Sindi has no delusions to bank upon. He is not "fortunate enough to have been born with their simpleness of mind" either. His existential drifting over the surface of the earth and his experimentation with the self only intensity his dismal loneliness and acute sense of meaninglessness of life. He tries to seek, finally, in detachment a solution to his problems.

The detachment which Sindi so resolutely cultivates to overcome his painful memories and meaninglessness of life becomes a source of deeper agony to him. It is his detachment that is responsible for the tragedy of Babu and June. Sindi's detachment does not seem to be wise. Explaining the reluctant transfer of her love to Babu, June tells Sindi :

"...You are so tied up with your own detachment it makes little difference whether you love or you don't." She further protests :

> I had wanted to belong to you but you didn't want it. You are so self-sufficient there is hardly any place for me in your life — except perhaps as a mistress (p. 158).

Obsession of Sindi with the notion of detachment makes him shirk his responsibility. Like Camus Meursault he is always bored with the world, and like Neil of Philip Roth's Good Bye, Columbus he does not want to shoulder even ordinary responsibilities. He muses if his detachment and objectivity have been of any value

3. *Ibid.*, p. 208.

in life. Detachment becomes a mysty notion with him and is used to mean so many things including love in a detached manner : "Love without fooling yourself that the things you love are indispensable either to you or to the world" (p. 170).

We find, in *The Strange Case of Billy Biswas*, Billy ceased to belong to the world after his physical disappearance into the jungles. He felt being impelled by

> a great force, urkraft, a... a primitive force. His Swedish friend Tulla had long ago sensed his primitive force in him. Even at the age of fourteen, while staying in Bhubaneshwar, he received the intimations of his primitive self : It was as though a slumbering part of me had suddenly come awake (p. 122).

He realized, "something has gone wrong with my life." The is where I belong. This is what I have always dreamt of. At that times however, he was not able to understand the source and the precise nature of this call. He says :

> I could not figure out what existed or troubled me unless it was a sudden interest in my own identity. Who was I? where had I come from? Where was I going? (p. 122).

Billy's experience just before he takes the momentous decision to make the final departure into the jungle on the second day of his expedition has mystic undertones and reminds us of Sidharth's renunciation of his wife and child. Billy felt as if "the inheritors of the cosmic night were waiting and walking and stairing" at him and he was the "first man on earth facing the earth's first night." His departure is for him a prelude to an arduous quest for something beyond himself. It is not an escape from life and its realities but an escape into what he considers to be the real life far from the madding crowd and the sordid, meaningless existence in the civilized world.

Billy does not find meaning of life either in white America or in the upper class Indian society. He tells Romi that he decided to live in Harlem because "that was the most human place he could find" and that "white America was much too civilized for him." He hates likewise "the upper crust of Indian society" which he himself comes from, for he finds it swarming with pompous and mixed up people :

> Aristically, they are as dry as dust. Intellectually they could do no better than mechanically mouth ideas that the West abandoned a generation ago (p. 197).

The terrible shock he feels at his degradation provokes his flight from meaningless civilized world. His alternatives are crystallized. He has two "clear choices" — either to "follow this call of the primitive, this vision, whatever the cost, or be condemned to total decay" (p. 190). He decides to go in for the first option.

Billy's search for meaning, however, is conducted in a very hostile atmosphere and he has to pay a heavy price for it. The sophisticated society, in its "middle-class mediocrity", makes it a point to bracket men like him with "irresponsible fools and common criminals" and does all that is possible to prevent them from "seeking such meagre fulfilment of their destiny as their tortured lives allowed" (pp. 231-32). Efforts to bring Billy back to civilization by capturing him by police force only lead to the final tragedy. He pays with his life for not conforming to the norms of the Urban civilization — for daring "to step out of its stifling confines."

Joshi's another novel *The Apprentice*, also depicts, through less exhaustively, the plight of the contemporary man, who is "sailling about in a confused society without norms, without direction, without even, perhaps a purpose" (p. 74).

Ratan's humiliating experience of job-hunting make him realize the cruelty of the human lot. He himself becomes "at the age of twenty-one, a hypocrite and a liar; in short, a sham." As a clerk he works "harder than almost anybody in the department except the superintendent himself'' (p. 37). Ratan is nevertheless always haunted by the morbid fear of losing his job and suffers from a keen desire for getting promotion and an intense preoccupation with work. He is almost invariably in a high strange mental condition, which threatens to ravage his soul and deprive him of his personality and identity. Ultimately he succumbs inescapably to the needs of his job and, rewarded with security and promotion, ends up by accepting a bribe when he needs money.

The Strange Case of Billy Biswas and *The Apprentice* suggest different approaches to counteract life's meaninglessness. As Billy's example testifies, if one is able to establish a rapport with the primitive force in the world of nature, one can get rid of all problems of life. Belasia, it is held, symbolizes "the primitive culture, the untapped subterranean resources of psychic energy." It would be better to regard her as the matter (Prakriti), which according to the Sankhya System of Indian Philosophy, is "One" and eternal, not an illusionary appearance but something real. Billy might be taken to represent the soul (Purusa), which by its mere presence excites Matter and illumines the processes of the evolution of the universe. Bilasia, we are reminded, is "the embodiment of that primal and invulnerable force that had ruled these [Maikala] hills, perhaps with earth, since time began." Her "enormous eyes", wc arc told, "poured out a sexuality that was nearly as primeval as the forest that surrounded them" (p 141). In the Sankhya Philosophy the material universe is traced to a First Cause.

In Joshi's last novel *The Last Labyrinth* the understanding born of suffering and humiliation that seems to have been presented as a solution to life's meaninglessness. The novelist suggests that a mere rational approach to life's problem will not do. Einstein once affirmed : "We have to jump out of our mind." The explanations given by thinkers like Darwin and Freud are only partially true. Frued, it is maintained, seems to be "groping in the night of man's mind" (p. 77). And Darwin's theory of evolution fails to give a plausible answer to certain queries regarding life and its riddles. Anuradha says : "May be Krishna begins where Drawin left off" (p. 132).

The search for a meaning is more clearly marked in the protagonist of *The Last Labyrinth*. Som Bhaskar needs to be assured that all is well :

> But I needed the trust — who doesn't? I needed it all the more because I did not trust myself, or my men, or my fate or the ceaseless travel on the social wheel (p. 63).

He is very anxious to know what he wants. The desire to know is a labyrinth :

> If only one knew what one wanted. or, may be, to know was what I wanted.To know. Just that. No more. No less. This, then, was a labyrinth, too, this going forward and backward and sideways of the mind (p. 53).

In Arun Joshi's novels too the awareness of self is inspired by a confrontation with some crisis or catastrophe — the death of June Blyth for Sindi, the seduction of Rima Kaul for Billy, the death of the Brigadier for Ratan Rathor and the death of Anuradha for Som Bhaskar.

One may establish a tenuous relation among different solutions put forth by Joshi, but there is no real progression of thought from novel to novel. He seems to be groping for the solution to face the meaninglessness of life, and his search for it, in its present state, remains indeterminate. His novels, nevertheless, go a long way to affirm the value of meaningfulness in life. They seem to indicate that one can realize the essence of life by liberating the self from the clutches of mercenary civilization and by paying due heed to authentic calls of the inner being. This seems to Joshi to be the only way out of saving man from terrifying degradation and purposelessness of the contemporary sordid, meaningless world.

6

Fictional Art and Visions

Arun Joshi marks a definite departure from the general run of Indian English novelists in many ways. His novels delineate more of human problems than issues arising out of regional loyalties. His characters step out of themselves and question not only the atmosphere which impinges on their consciousness but their own self-indulgent attitudes keeping them away from facing the truth. His condemnation of the industrial, the civilized and the materialistic world is not guided by a sentimental extolling of Indian philosophy and values of life but by a genuine faith in the integrity of the primitive values of sensuousness, passion and action. His technique of elf-introspection intensified by self-mockery opens a new dimension in the art of Indian English fiction.

The Foreigner, Arun Joshi's first novel, is written in the form of things past. The narration keeps moving from the recent past in Boston to the present in Delhi. Joshi has a vast range and makes a novel out of the wide variety of scenes. During the course of the novel, he takes us to Nairobi where Sindi, the central character as well as the narrator of the story was born, to London where he studied; to a night club in Soho where he worked as a dishwasher and barman; to Scotland where he worked at a small village library and discussed religion, God and mysticism with a Catholic priest; to Boston where he studied for six years and met June and Babu and to Delhi where he ultimately settled down. Despite his desclaimer, "I am not very good at remembering events."

The novel opens like a thriller with the scene set in a morgue where Sindi identifies the dead body of his friend Babu Rao

Khemka who has been killed in a car accident on Mass Turnpike. Subsequently he goes to June and, over a cup of coffee in a restaurant, breaks the news of Babu's death.

Sindi is a humane person who sympathizes with Babu, June and Sheila when they are in trouble. As an employee of the foreign student centre, Sindi takes charge of Babu when he arrives in Boston to join college. When Babu fails in his exams. Sindi meets the Dean in order to save Babu from being thrown out of the college. Later, when June informs him that she is carrying Babu's child and seeks his help and advice, Sindi decides to marry June. In a bid to be away from her, he had left Boston and taken up a job in New York. But now he decides to give up his philosophy of detachment. He goes to Boston but only to learn that June had died in the course of an operation for abortion. June's death leads to his realization of the fallacy of detachment.

The Strange Case of Billy Biswas, like Conrad's *Lord Jim*, is narrated from the witness-narrator's point of view. The narrator in this novel is Romi (Romesh Sahai), a friend of the protagonist Billy (Bimal Biswas) whom he met as a student in New York. Like Marlow in *Lord Jim*, Romi performs the task as an involved friend and as a detached narrator. Both become more and more involved as the novel progress; both follow the take to the end. And they have another feature in common. Throughout the narrative, Marlow repeatedly asserts that he was not able to comprehend Jim fully :

> He (Jim) was not —
> if I may so clear to me
> He was not clear.[1]

Similarly, Romi disclaims in the beginning of the narrative that he has understood Billy :

> As I grow old, I realize that the most futile cry
> of man is his impossible wish to be understood.
> The attempt to understand is even more futile. If
> in spite of this I propose to relate Billy's story, it

1. Joseph Conard, *Lord Jim* (New York : Doubleday, 1925), p. 177.

> is not so much because I claim to have understood him as it is on account of a deep and unrelieved sense of wonder that in the middle of the twentieth century, in the heart of Delhi's smart society, there should have lived a man of such extraordinary obsessions (p. 7).

Billy is a man of brilliant intellect, profound sensibility and extraordinary obsession. He belongs to a rich respectable family, his father being a judge of India's Supreme Court and expects him to take up engineering as a career and Billy does go to America for a degree in Engineering. However, he earns his Ph.D. in Anthropology because that is his first love. Billy is basically an anthropologist and studies deeply the tribal attitudes and customs. He feels deeply interested in the places described in the books he reads. In fact his whole life is organised around his interest in the primitive man.

In order to cure his obsession for the primitive and to settle down in life, Billy decides to get married. He hopes that marriage would restrain him. However, his marriage to Meena, a sophisticated and most beautiful girl of his own Bengali community, is not a success. Meena tries her best to understand Billy but his interest in the wild exasperates her. As Billy himself says :

> The more I tried to tell her what was corroding me, bringing me to the edge of despair so to speak, the more resentful she became (p. 185).

Billy forsakes meaningless existence in the civilized world because he feels choked by the phony atmosphere of the modern society. He rejects the artificiality, hollowness and snobbery of the sophisticated people. As he analyses it later :

> What got me was the superficiality, the same of values. I don't think all city societies are as shallow as ours. I am, of course, talking mainly of the so-called upper classes. I did not really get to know the others (pp. 178-79).

Billy finds his fulfilment and essence of human existence in the primitive tribal life. He likes living with the foresters because they are not materialistic : "Nobody here is interested in the prices of foodgrains or new seeds or roads or elections and stuff like that" (p. 113). He likes the unrestrained life style of the primitive people who go in for uninhibited drinking and dancing and open orgiastic love-making.

Billy's union with Bilasia makes him discover "that bit of himself that he has searched for all his life and without which his life is nothing more than the poor reflection of a million others" (p. 142).

In *The Foreigner*, Joshi had moved from Boston to New Delhi. In *The Strange Case of Billy Biswas*, he moves from New Delhi to Satpura Hills in Madhya Pradesh. The two geographic locations represent two different cultures — the sophisticated and the primitive. Billy's unconscious self drives him to renounce the monotonous respectability of his high middle-class society and seek his roots in the company of a primitive tribe. The sophisticated Meena represents New Delhi's anglicized ruling-class immersed in the phoney materialism whereas the primitive Bilasia represents the Satpura bhils.

Ratan Rathor, the protagonist in *The Apprentice*, is the narrator who "Must tell all. All or nothing. What use is a confession is not total." Clamence tells his story to a Frenchman — the person sitting at the next table in the bar. He attempts to open up conversation thus :

> May I, Monsieur, offer my services without running the risk of intruding? (p. 21).

Ratan also tells his lifetable to a silent listener — a young student who has come from Punjab to Delhi to rehearse for the N.C.C. Parade on the Republic Day. Replying to a probable query about the direction to reach the grounds, Ratan finds the young student to be a fit listener to his tale : "or, if you could wait a little I shall drop you. I go the same way. Can you wait? Good." Like Coleridge's *Ancient Mariner*, Ratan insists that the listener hear him out. Ratan also reminds us of Marlow, the first person narrator in Conrad's *Youth*, who tells in retrospect the tale of his youth to a group of listeners. *The Apprentice*, like *The Strange*

Case of Billy Biswas, is rendered in chronological fashion, with sporadic flash-backs interspersing it.

The Apprentice is set in India familiar to the Urban middle-class. Ratan Rathor is both the hero as well as the anti-hero of the novel. Though he does not feel at home in society, he does not abandon it as Billy Biswas had done. Interestingly, he embodies the very world of material values which his predecessors Sindi Oberoi and Billy Biswas had rejected. He is neither a rebel nor a dissident; he is a victim. After feeling alienated from society, he adopts himself to the ways of the world. He has a powerful instinct for survival. He knows that some people survive through defiance while others do through their ability. And there are still others who servive by Sycophancy and by being survile to those in power. Ratan fully succumbs to the worldly pleasures. At every stage he puts up an initial resistance only to discover the futility of his endeavour like so many of his kind for nobody seemed to know :

> What was right? what was wrong?
> ...that was where the rub lay (p. 64).

Ratan is a child of double inheritance; the idealhood of his father is matched by the pragmatism of his mother. He is greatly inspired by his father's active participation in the country's freedom movement. He was only ten years old when his father, responding to the call of Mahatma Gandhi, abandoned his practice as a lawyer and gave away most of his wealth to join the revolutionaries. Once as he stood at the head of procession of freedom fighters, he was gunned down by a British Sergeant. The incident which Ratan had witnessed, made on indelible impression on his mind.

Though Ratan progresses upward in rank, he becomes increasingly fraudulent and unscruplous : "The more money I accumulated, the more I was dissatisfied and the more I was determined to 'enjoy' life.'' He confesses that he has become a "master faker." He has added a new dimension to his life, and he has become, at the age of twenty-one, a hypocrite and a liar. He aquires a sense of docility and obedience. He readily accepts bribes and now owns a car, a flat, a refrigerator and also has twenty thousand rupees in the bank.

The most striking change in Ratan is his sudden interest in wine and women's so far he had lacked the courage to give vent to his desires. But now he ogles at the women around : "I felt bold, unfettered. I started at them, the women. Openly, Wilfully" (p. 77). Not only this, he visits prostitutes. In short Ratan is "at the peak of the dung heap that I had been climbing all my life" (p. 85).

Ratan's morality is so completely eroded that he cannot bring himself to confess before the authorities. He visits the temple to seek peace and courage but he meets a priest who is ready to grease his palm to save the skin of his son, a contractor who having used sub-standard material in the construction resulting in the collapse of many roofs was facing punishment. He concludes that even religion is not free from corruption and no succour can be drawn from it. The novelist presents an India riddled with corruptions. God can be propitiated by gifts in black money to his temples, where the priest themselves are as corrupt as the narrator.

The latest novel of Arun Joshi, *The Last Labyrinth*, continues in the tradition of the first person singular. The narrator hero is Som Bhaskar, a wealthy young industrialist, who relates the events of his life in flashback. Like the heroes of *The Foreigner* and *The Strange Case of Billy Biswas*, Som belongs to the upper strata of society and his quest of life too, like theirs, is for the meaning of life.

Som flits from one pleasure to another; he becomes the incarnation of the quest of hunger for the joy of life. He therefore goes in search of new experience whether they concern business or fornication. But ironically, far from attaining a sense of fulfilment, he has a terrible sense of emptiness of voids within and voids without. Everything in this mysterious world, he finds, is "a haze."

Anuradha exercises such an overpowering fascination over Som that he neglects his business, his family and his health in an effort to win her. He makes frequent trips to Benaras and is determined to aquire her for himself, his soul and body. And Geeta, his own wife, is all that a wife could be — trusting, beautiful and well-bred. She shows tremendous loyalty and courage in standing by him despite his erratic conduct. And yet, Som is drawn in to an aching, painful obsessive love for Anuradha.

All his life Som seeks someone who has the capacity to resolve the contradictions of his life. He does not find it in his wife, nor in Leela Sabnis, the clever young professor who could readily quote from Freud or Descartes : "Oh yes, Leela Sabnis knew a lot." She is scholar, an M.A. and Ph.D. from Michigan, something else from London. She is married and divorced. Her husband, she claimed proudly, divorced her for reading too much.

Though Som has sex with Anuradha, and earlier with Leela Sabnis, he is not happy because of his spiritual hollowness. He does not attempt to resolve the contradictions of life through faith. He fails to sublimate his desires from the animalistic to the spiritual; he becomes a spokesman for Westernized Indian aristocracy which has lost his spiritual roots. A mere rational approach to life as represented by Western-educated and affluent Som, is not sufficient. The labyrinth of life can be resolved through intuition and faith rather than science and reason.

The novelist's vision of life, his compassion and sensibility are manifested in the archetypal patterns of conflict between good and evil which is typically Indian. The crime manifested is amended in the protagonist's mind itself which is a hundred times more forceful a punishment than what Courts of Law can inflict. Hence, the confession before a student who himself is an apprentice is more appropriate than what it should have been if it had been done before any authority.

Arun Joshi's success in handling his seemingly flimsy material stands within the framework of his novel. His preoccupation with social and personal blemishes is made all the more attractive solely because of the autobiographical retrospective narrative of Ratan Rathor which traces in a convincing manner the growth and development of the protagonist's character. It casts a spell on the reader as it does on the imaginative companion. It throws light on the fact that human corruption will always provide a built-in-tension and duality in the scheme of things which enlighten the novelist's view on the psychological, moral, and mythical aspects of life. Yet Joshi does not aim at conveying any message.

Like Ratan Rathor, his problem is that of educating himself in order to survive "this deluge of progress." The story is being told in retrospect keeping more or less the chronological order. In *The Apprentice* Arun Joshi makes clear that mere surviving of "bourgeois filth" does not solve much of the problems, and that an involvement with the mankind in the right sense is what is particularly essential.

Thus, the short study of Arun Joshi's *The Apprentice* focused mainly on the art and vision. Trends in recent fiction unmistakably indicate how new novelists like Arun Joshi is trying new paths and this is the surest sign of the continued vitality of the art in the hands of Indian writers writing in English. They believe that they can no longer employ conventional plots, for modern life emposes upon the novelists considerable physical, mental and intellectual strain. Hence, quest has become the leitmotif of modern fiction, quest to "create a symphony of meaning out of the epiphanies of life."[2]

Joshi's protagonists are singularly individualistic and completely self-centered. Though highly educated — some of them having studied abroad — their behaviour is incompatible with the natural laws of everyday reality. They violate norms of social life and indulge in actions which are instinctive, and irrational. Alienated from the sinister, materialistic life around them, they try to work out their destiny in their own way. Though successful in freeing themselves from the restraints of their external environment, they remain subjected by the urges of their sub-conscious self. Their seemingly independent actions are in fact the results of the dictates of their "Id", the fountain-head of their uncontrolled basic instincts and sub-conscious desires. Juxtaposed with the banal

2. Hari Mohan Prasad, ''Dimensions of Realism in Indo-English Fiction'', *The Indian Journal of English Studies*, XXI (1981-92), p. 140.

reality of the life around, this fantastic provides a double vision of fantasy and reality in his novels and makes them compellingly gripping stories from start to the end.

Thus, we come to the conclusion that Arun Joshi's novels are increasingly bold attempts to discover the meaning of life. They try to devise ways and means for eliminating the discrepancy between the individual's pursuits and his fulfilment. Joshi's heroes are lonely and misfits in the world in which they have to live and face the meaninglessness of life. Though they are not religious or saintly, they are humble enough to learn lessons taught to them by life's problems. While experiencing the normal claims of love and hatred, doubts and dilemmas, they try to face challenges of their meaningless life by outstripping the narrow confines of their distraught selves.

Joshi suggests a different solution in each of his novels. He does not care to work out fully the philosophical possibilities of his themes. Nor does he try to probe deeply into his character's psychology. There is nothing very original about the means suggested by him to counteract life's meaninglessness; they have been described in Indian philosophy and scriptures elaborately, but the way he integrates them in his novels is really remarkable.

7

Conclusion

In course of time as confidence increased the novelists came to feel that they could satisfactorily use novel as a capable medium for introspection and self-analysis. As the cultural conflicts between the West and the East had been quite pervasive it was found to be ingrained in the personality of the nation. It was visible not only in domestic habits or sartorial concerns but also in beliefs and convictions. This interaction was by and large interpreted as a clash till 1947 and the feeling that one was an exploiter and the other exploited or that one was pragmatic and the other idealistic continued to dominate the Indian mind. This was the clash of two different mental attitudes which Kipling had referred to when he had said : "The twain shall never meet." But it will be wrong to presume that there was no amalgam of the two cultures or there was no attempt to reconcile the two. From this point of view two novels of Arun Joshi, *The Foreigner* and *The Strange Case of Billy Biswas* are significant as they deal with alienation of displaced persons felt both at social and domestic levels. 'The Foreigner' tells the story of Sindi Oberoi, a young man who feels alienated in his own country. But his alienation is not so much geographical or physical as spiritual as it is born of a crisis of conscience. He could not therefore, develop any emotional attachment to any place. Caught up in the trap of a corrupt wealthy industrialist he found himself provoked, but finally decided to continue his association with the concern for the sake of the poor labourers. This was his another gesture on his part to establish contact with the society in which he has been living and find a meaning in his existence. But probably even this was a decision of the moment, not a futuristic view or commitment to a view of life.

It is difficult to pinpoint and spell out the values that guide the life of geographically displaced persons. Sindi Oberoi, the persona of the narrator did not have any definite morality. He did not believe in the institution of marriage, nor did he think much of love, friendship or loyalty in the International context. Only the sincerity of attachment could be the acid test of human relationships for him. But the irony was that even this existential anguish failed to direct his life in any definite direction. Right from the time of his birth things had just happened to him. Even his visit to India was a matter of chance : he had tossed a coin to decide as to whether he should accept the job in Nigeria or India. For him life was a more collection of successive decisions. He explained his tragedy of helplessness :

> You have faith in yourself as a free agency,
> I have lost even that (p. 82).

Another such strange person is the central character of *The Strange Case of Billy Biswas.* Son of judge of the Supreme Court, Billy Biswas fell in love with Bilasia a tribal beauty and did not return for about ten years. His wife and father ultimately took the help of the police to capture and bring him back home. But while attempting to run away he got killed by a constable. This story of Billy Biswas is presented by his collector friend who had no fascination for his job. In his approach to the problems and attraction for the tribals he shows the elitist outlook. So what he was examining as a central thing was the difference between the tribals and the civilised persons. He knew that the unimaginative society could not but deal with Billy in the same way as it disposes of "revolutionaries, seers and lovers" (p. 240).

It is also very remarkable to note when Mr. Khemka, the Indian businessman asked Sindi Oberoi, "why are you so stranger?" the later said :

> I'm not strange. I am perhaps different from
> you and your world. My set of experiences has

> taught me a reality that is different from yours (p. 142).

This applies to Billy Biswas also. He was strange because he had not cared to fulfil the expectations of his society by accepting to live by its standards. It is clear that for giving precedence to experience over the established social norms both the narrator and his friend Billy were condemned. The maximum the narrator could do was to present his ironic attitude in novelistic form and thus play the role of a helpless spectator. He was condemned to live amidst the heaps of his frustrated dreams and hopes like his friend Billy.

Once again in *The Apprentice*, the third novel of Arun Joshi, has been presented, of course, on a larger convas — this helplessness of man. Ratan Rathor, the narrator, is a living example of the principle of expediency. Mediocre and unambitious, he held out a very high position in the government in course of time. But as he went higher he felt more confident of his security and capable of betraying his nation for pittance. He says :

> So you see, my friend, here I am, a man without honour : a man without shame. Perhaps a man of our time. But there I go again... (p. 147).

Ratan's father was a freedom fighter, but he himself was a self centred man. Compared to his father who had sacrificed his honour and even life at the altar of freedom, Ratan Rathor was a helpless creature. So with all his skill in manupulating the files and official success he rightly felt that he was sitting on top of a dung-hill. There cannot be any scope for idealism or utopian vision when the pillars of administration are ministers, secretaries and brokers.

Several other novelists have also depicted the clash of cultures or unadjusted lives of foreign trained Indians. B. Rajan's *The Dark Dancer* is a good example. But the intensity and understanding with which Arun Joshi presents this discords is unique, it is without a precedent. In the same way some novelists have dwelt on the experiences of the native aliens — Raja Rao's *The Serpent and the Rope* (1960) is an example but Kamla Markandaya's *The Nowhere Man* (1972) is different in tone and tenor. Kamla Markandaya, herself an Indian, has married an English man and lives in England. R.P. Jhabvala's autobiography *An Experience in India* (1972) bears testimony to this feeling of rootlessness and maladjustment. Another novel, Anita Desai's *Bye-Bye Black Bird* (1971) is weak variation on the theme of racial arrogance and consequent alienation of outsiders. On the life of expatriates has come out another novel *The Marriage* (1973) Timeri Murari underlines the feeling that the relationships of Indians Englishmen although spread over years cannot be intimate. As their relationships are based on selfish interests they will never be deep. *The Marriage* is naturalistic depiction of reality.

It has been pointed out that the life of expatriates is replete with the feeling of loneliness. But it is not necessary to be an expatriate to experience isolation. Anita Desai has attempted to show in *Where Shall We Go This Summer* (1975) that even in family where there is no cause for worry there can be the feeling of boredom and allegation. Sita is a tolerably beautiful woman of forty, has four children, and is expecting the fifth very soon. She has a loving and understanding husband. But she feels terribly lonely as she finds her life without a challenge. She started smoking heavily to escape the ennui but did not find it efficacious.

The creative work of the young writer, Arun Joshi, is developing along the course of existentialism. Sindi Oberoi, the main character of his first novel, *The Foreigner* is an existential character. He compares himself with a tree without roots. He is an orphan, his parents perished in an aircraft accident when he was only four. He feels himself a stranger everywhere in Boston, in Kenya where he was born, in London where he was educated and in Idia, the land of his ancestors, where he has come back only because it is a good place to forget himself as any other. His estrangement is explained by his "fate as an orphan," change of places and by many other things. It creates spiritual depression in his soul; everything in the world is alien to him, but he can get rid of his own self.

Sindi's pessimistic attitude is aggravated by the fact that he does not have faith in anything, neither in God, nor in the motherland, nor in revolution, nor in love. He does not have any ideals. Nihilism of Sindi is manifested not only in disbelief in social progress but also in his disbelief in the opportunity of personal happiness.

In the novel two 'triangles' have been introduced which cannot be classified as pertaining to love. Sindi is not capable of sincerity and deep feelings. Egoism of his nature is invincible. The first triangle of the protagonists (June, Sindi, Sheila) very much resembles the triangle in Raja Rao's novel *The Serpent and the Rope* (Madeliene, Ramaswamy, Savitri). The theme is the same, the situation is also the same, but the decision is entirely different. Raja Rao's hero is overwhelmed with feelings, while Arun Joshi's egoist is the embodiment of indifference.

The other 'triangle' is Sindi, June, Babu Rao. Although Sindi continues to meet June, he does not object against Babu Rao's courting her here and there. When Babu comes to know that June loves Sindi, he prefers to disappear from life. After the news of his death, June, who is carrying a child from him, decides in despair to undergo an abortion in hospital and during the operation she dies. It is too late for Sindi to realise that he is guilty of the death of both and he is seized with belated repentance :

> Wouldn't Babu still be living if I have not
> surrendered my body to June that night we went
> for a ride? ...And if Babu had not killed himself
> June would still be living (p. 196).

After such an unexpected, almost simultaneous death of two young people, Sindi goes away to India and tries to fill up the spiritual vaccum by studies of Indian Philosophy, but all in vain.

Arun Joshi thus uses the image of a foreigner as a myth. In all his novels his heroes act as foreigners either to the environment or to themselves. They are foreigners because they are exposed either by their sensibility, lack of identification with the world around or a knowledge of themselves. Joshi uses this motif so extensively that it takes on the character of a myth. Sindi is a foreigner in the fullest sense of the world. Billy is a foreigner because he can't identify himself with the society of which he is a product. Ratan has knowledge of himself without discrimination and resolution. Sindi is against both Eastern and Western materialism. Billy likes the tribals because they are unmaterialistic and nearer nature. The whole career of Ratan is a severe indictment of the materialistic world.

The long tedious journey of Arun Joshi's protagonists helps them to arrive at some meaning. The sense of guilt that has oppressed Sindi ever since Babu committed suicide is erased with the traumatic realization that Babu's father is a cheat of great magnitude. The satisfaction he has at end from the uniqueness of having just one book enables him to settle his account with the past. His eyes are opened to the miseries of the world and he arrives at a re-adjustment of his values. Having become a sort of "Karmayogi" he finds his equanimity and salvation in the land of his birth. Though Billy is shot dead and his search, like that of *querry* of Graham Green's *A Burnt Out Case* and *Murphy* of Beckett's Murphy, is interrupted and ultimately terminated by death, he attains self-fulfilment in the midst of the tribals. He experiences their joys and sorrows, living their beliefs and superstitions while the tribal people soon start adoring him as their king and God. He becomes some sort of a priest. He finds his fulfilment in the love of Bilasia the essence of that primitive force that had called him night after night, year after year. He arrives at a parting of the ways in his life and takes the path that leads him to his salvation first in love and then in death. Ratan Rathor too finds meaning in his apprenticeship *i.e.*, wiping the shoes of the congregation outside the temple. He is learning to be of use and he knows that the smell of his hands would prevent him from going astray. No more an island, he realizes the truth of what his father used to tell him — whatever you do touches someone somewhere. As an apprentice in more ways than one, he has now realized his identity as a small, humble drop in the ocean of the world. However, "petrified" our civilization may be, there is hope as long as man is willing to learn, as Ratan Rathor himself has learnt, as he wants his listeners to learn. The novel rightly ends with a dawn which is both outward and inward, though it is a cold one.

✪

Bibliography

Primary Source

Joshi, Arun, *The Foreigner*, Hind Pocket Books, New Delhi, 1968.

Joshi, Arun, *The Stange Case of Billy Biswas*, Hind Pocket Books, New Delhi, 1971.

Joshi, Arun, *The Apprentice*, Orient Paperbacks, New Delhi, 1974.

Joshi, Arun, *The Last Labyrinth*, Orient Paperbacks, New Delhi, 1981.

Secondary Source

Alienation, *Concept Term and Meanings* (NewYork and London Seminar Press, 1973).

Alien Voice, *Perspectives on Commonwealth Literature*, edited by Avdhesh K. Srivastva, Print House, Lucknow, 1981.

Asnani, Shyam M., *A Study of Arun Joshi's Fiction*, The Literary Half-Yearly, XIX, 2 (July 1978).

Banerjee, Purabi, *A Winner's Secrets*, An Interview with Purabi Banerjee, *The Sunday Statesman*, 27, February 1983.

Ball, Eklund Jane, *The Range of Literature Fiction* (Boston : Houghton Miffin).

Bachelord, Gaston, *The Poetics of Reverie*, Childhood Language and Cosmos, trans. Daniel Russell (Boston : Beacon Press, 1971).

Bhatnagar, O.P., *Arun Joṣhi's The Foreigner* : A critic of East and West. *JIWE*, Vol. I, No. 2, July 1973.

The Art and vision of Arun Joshi : Recent Revelations of Indian Fiction in English, published by Prakash Book Depot, Bareily, 1983.

Barnes, E. Hazel, *The Literature of Possibility : A Study in Humanistic Extentialism*, Tavistock Publication, London, 1961.

Bose, A., *Indian Writing in English*, ed. K.N. Sinha, The University of Bihar, Muzaffarpur.

Conard Joseph, *Lord Jim* (London : Hazel Waston and Viney Ltd., 1900).

——, *Lord Jim* (New York : Doubleday 1925).

Camus Albert, *The Collected Fiction* (London : Hamish Hamilton, 1962).

Dhawan, R.K., *The Fictional World of Arun Joshi*, Classical Publishing Company, New Delhi, 1986.

Desai, Anita, *Bye-Bye Black Bird*, 1971.

——, *Where Shall We Go This Summer*, 1975.

Harvey W.J., *Character and The Novel* (London : Chatto and Windus, 1965).

Joshi, Arun, *The Survivor*, in Modern Indian Short Story : An Anthology, ed. Suresh Kohli (New Delhi, Arnold Heinemann,1974).

Jain, Jasbir, *Foreigners and Strangers : Arun Joshi's Heroes*, The Journal of Indian Writing in English, 5/1, January 1977).

Jhabwala, R.P., *An Experience in India*, 1972.

Mathur, O.P., *The Existential Note on Arun Joshi*; *Commonwealth Quarterly*, Vol. 5, December, 1980.

——, *From Existentialism to Karmayoga : A study of Arun Joshi's The Foreigner*; *The Alien Voice*, ed. A.K. Srivastva, Print House, Lucknow (U.P.), 1981.

Mukharjee, Meenakshi, *The Twice Born Fiction* : *Themes and Techniques of the Indian Novel in English* (New Delhi : Heinemann Educational Books, 1971).

Maugham, W.S., *Razor's Edge* (Philadelphia : Blackiston Co. 1944).

——, *The Summing Up* (New York : The New American Library, 1938).

Markandaya, Kamala, *The Nowhere Man*, 1972.

Murary Timeri, *The Marriage*, 1973.

Man in Modern Fiction (New York : Random House, 1958).

N. Radhakrishan, ed. Arun Joshi : *A Study of His Fiction*, Gandhi Gram, Tamilnadu, 1984.

Narasimhaiya, C.D., *A Note From The Third World Towards The Redefinition of Culture*, Awakened Conscience, New Delhi.

Naik, M.K., "The Political Novel in Indian Writing in English; *Politics and The Novel in India*, ed. Yogendra K. Malik (Orient Longman, 1978).

——, *A History of Indian English Literature* (Sahitya Academy, New Delhi, 1982).

Nandi Pritish, *Literature of Protest* (Aspects of Indian Literature, 1975).

Prasad, Hari Mohan, *Dimensions of Realism in Indo-English Fiction*, The Indian Journal of English Studies, XXI (1981-82).

——, *Arun Joshi*, Arnold Heinemann, New Delhi, 1985.

Rajan, B., *The Dark Dancer*.

Rao, Raja, *The Serpent and The Rope,* 1980.

Rao, C. Malathi, *The Foreigner : Arun Joshi*, The Literary Criterion, 8, No. 4 (Summer, 1969).

Reply to M.R. Dua, dated September 3, 1971.

Reply to V. Gopal Reddy, dated January 8, 1981.

Rao, A.V. Krishna, The Indo-Anglian Novel and the Changing Tradition, Mysore, 1972.

Singh, R.A., *The Existential Characters of Arun Joshi and Anita Desai*, Prakash Book Depot, 1990 : *The Foreigner*: A Study, PBD Bareily, 1991.

Singh, Dr. R.S., *The Novel of India*, Sterling Publication, Delhi.

Sartre, Jean Paul, *Being and Nothingness*, translated Hazel E. Banes (New York), Washington, Squre Press, Pocket Books, (1966).

——, *Existentialism and Humanism*, translated Philip Mairut (London), Methuin and Co. Ltd. 1948.

——, *Nausea*, translated R. Baldock, 1985.

Sharma, D.R., *The Fictional World of Arun Joshi*, The Indian Pen, 41, Nos. 9-10 (1977).

Srinath, C.N., *The Fiction of Arun Joshi*, The Literary Criterion, XII, Nos. 2 & 3 (1976).

——, *Crisis of Identity*, Assertion and Withdrawal in Naipul's and Arun Joshi, The Literary Criterion, 14/1 (1979).

——, *The Dairy of a Writer*, translated Boris Brasol (New York), 1954.

Tillich Paul, *The Courage to Be* (New Heaven : Yale University Press, 1952).

"The Hyptonized People", *Partisan Review*, 27/2 (1960).

The Spiritual Crisis of Man (London : Rider and Co., 1952).

The Sen Society (New York : Holt, Rinehart, 1955).

Verghese, C. Paul, *Problem of the Indian Creative Writers in English*, (Bombay : Somaiya Publication, 1971).

Wilson, Colin, *The Outsider* (Pen Books, London, 1956).